Measures of Truth

Newcastle Poetry Prize
Anthology 2020

Measures of Truth - Newcastle Poetry Prize Anthology 2020
Hunter Writers Centre Inc. and the University of Newcastle
Newcastle NSW 2300

Email: publishing@hunterwriterscentre.org
Published by
Hunter Writers Centre Inc. and the University of Newcastle
hunterwriterscentre.org
facebook.com/HunterWritersCentre

ISBN-978-0-6488504-1-0

Cover design by Gillian Humphries
Typesetting by HWC Publishing
2020 Published by Hunter Writers Centre Inc.

© Each poem is copyright of the respective author
© This collection copyright of Hunter Writers Centre

All rights reserved.
No part of this publication may be reproduced, stored in a retrieval system, or transmitted in any form by any means electronic, mechanical, photocopying, recording or otherwise without the prior consent of the publishers.

Nothing is ever hidden from the Earth

~ Damen O'Brien
Measures of Truth
Winner 2020 Newcastle Poetry Prize

Introduction

The Newcastle Poetry Prize, one of the country's most prestigious and important awards, is always a challenge for the judges. The thirty-six poems featured in this anthology have something to say about our times. They impressed us with their technique, surprised us with their language, moved us, made us laugh, and astounded us with their intellectual depth.

There are always themes and subjects that will be popular in any given year, and this year was no exception. Poems about the bushfires, climate change, the pandemic and its ensuing disruptions and mental health toll were very prevalent. Indeed, it would have been alarming if poets had ignored these topics. Poetry should address the Zeitgeist and express it, not in standard terms or as propaganda, but with that brilliance of idea, language and structure that makes us value a poem from any time, on any theme. There were also poems which dealt with the onset of ageing, dementia, the remembrance of parents and grandparents. Remembrance of what is no longer with us is often assumed to be inherently poetic, but poetry must do more than simply recall. It needs to shape that act of remembering into something more than nostalgic melancholy. Something far more vital. There were also several ekphrastic poems, a haul of poems about fishing, and for some reason, an album's worth of poems about music: classical composers, the Rolling Stones, Leonard Cohen and groupies all featured.

Of course, there is always a huge variation in the quality of the poems submitted. There are always a number of poems which show that the writer has little idea of how to construct a poem and little knowledge of what has been going on in contemporary poetry and whose main purpose is to instruct through rhyming statements and express a number of cliched feelings about the state of the world. These poems lack the specific and concentrated tools of poetry that would have enabled an intense connection with language.

Then there are the more ambitious pieces, competent but ultimately dissatisfying, because they are overwritten, extended beyond the writer's capacity to keep the reader's interest. One of the challenges of this unique prize is its length and many writers seem determined to draw out their poems to the allotted 200 lines whether the subject matter requires it or not. A number of entries became too attenuated for their own good. Some poems composed of sections just did not hang together in a compelling way or seemed cobbled together without an overarching coherence or vision.

Then there are those masterful pieces that achieve depth and resonance, which have an urgency that does not founder or fade, but which is sustained and developed throughout the duration of the poem. These are the poems which the judges read and reread many times, and which make the judging process wonderfully enjoyable and instructive. We feel these qualities are reflected most significantly in the winning pieces of course, but also in the anthology generally.

In creating poetry, you need to surrender to the poem, that is, to let it open a spaciousness inside you. When you surrender to the poem it means that the poem can take a turn anywhere, it can border on the unexpected and the unknown. The poems we have selected for the anthology we believe have achieved this level of success.

We'd like to thank the poets for giving us memorable work and such a high-quality reading experience. Congratulations to the winners for their superb poems. Thanks also to Hunter Writers Centre for the hard work of administering the prize and to the University of Newcastle for sponsorship of this unique and significant project.

1st Prize: Measures of Truth

This poem wowed us with its range of ideas from history, science, and philosophy. It posed big questions about the nature of truth: how can it be trusted or revealed, are some forms of truth more reliable than others, is truth simply relative to the available and existing levels of knowledge? These are complex questions which the poem deals with in very considered and forensically detailed ways. The poem is imaginative and wide-ranging and full of intriguing metaphors that speak of the complexity and strangeness of the nature of truth. The poem rewards multiple readings, which always afford new discoveries. The language is sophisticated and highly attuned, its level of craft and execution extremely impressive. The poem, constructed from five-lined stanzas of mostly twelve syllables, maintains its interest over the full length of the work. The poet's ability to build a sequence into a beautifully weighted whole is masterful.

2nd Prize: Keepers

We felt this was the best poem we had read about the recent Australian bushfires. The poem achieves great power by focussing on the experience of the fires of one particular group: bee-keepers. Tightly constructed of short lines whirling down the page like smoke, the poem wastes not a single word. The poem's precise sounds and visual imagery, its astute discernment and loving attention paid to syntax and to the cadences of the lines, result in a beautiful composition. The poem demonstrates that the magic of the poetry is inseparable from its risks, that this risk is a necessary component as it performs that balancing act between reality and the imaginative force at work within the poem. The poem's elegant, sensual mode combined with its emotional intensity creates great resonance.

3rd Prize: The Long Jetty Ghazals

This poem cleverly uses the Persian/Indian traditional form of the ghazal, though without the refrains and with more loosely rhymed couplets. It captures a place and time (Long Jetty on the central coast of New South Wales) and the time is now, with the pandemic hovering in the background, the town quieter than usual, and a sense of life in abeyance. Each couplet stands on its own as a miniature poem, just as they should in a ghazal. There is also a combination of lyrical imagery and a laconic, characteristically Australian, sense of humour. Beyond the light touch and good humour, the poem explores indigenous history and discovers that it is a living history in the town. The long-line couplets are also a nicely chosen form, mirroring the long jetties that the town is named for.

Commended: Groupie Acapella

An internally rhymed romp through rock and roll groupiedom, this poem is full of wit and vitality with a touch of pathos. The three-line stanzas are built for pace and movement and demonstrate skilful control of form. The poem impressively orchestrates the tensions between the personal and the public, love and infatuation, innocence and wisdom. The vernacular immediacy, ease of style, imagistic freshness and perspectives give this poem immediate appeal. Its wit and emotional resonances are well-sustained.

Commended: The Light We Convert

This sequence in twelve parts is an extended meditation on western classical music and the nature of art. It shows immaculate technique and clever use of rhyme and metre. The poem has clarity without sacrificing complexity. The poem is highly textured, the tonal keys are adroitly played as the poet lets the registers dip and slide with maximum effect. Here the poet skilfully finds the forms, movements, and verbal constructions to enact and embody the poem's well-nuanced perceptions.

Mike Ladd
Judith Beveridge

THE UNIVERSITY OF NEWCASTLE
AUSTRALIA

2020 Newcastle Poetry Prize Winners

Winner 2020 Newcastle Poetry Prize
Measures of Truth - Damen O'Brien

2nd Prize
Keepers - Anthony Lawrence

3rd Prize
The Long Jetty Ghazals - Robert Edmonds

Commended
The Light We Convert - Alex Skovron

Commended
Groupie Acapella - Julie Manning

Hunter Writers Centre Award
the bees - Christopher (Kit) Kelen

Harri Jones Memorial Prize
Rock Hopping - Peter Ramm

Local Award
The Ways You Haven't Left Me - Judy Johnson

Contents

Measures of Truth   13
Damen O'Brien

Keepers   19
Anthony Lawrence

The Long Jetty Ghazals   23
Robert Edmonds

The Light We Convert   28
Alex Skovron

Groupie Acapella   34
Julie Manning

the bees   40
Christopher (Kit) Kelen

Rock Hopping   51
Peter Ramm

The Ways You Haven't Left Me   54
Judy Johnson

The Island in the Roundabout   60
Chris Andrews

Nudged   63
Rod Usher

Isolations   64
Paul Hetherington

Annotations   67
John Foulcher

Feral   72
James Lucas

The Book of Crow   76
Steve Evans

They   80
Catherine Wright

In Perugia, November 1, 2007   82
Oliver Driscoll

draft [1] [two]   85
Christine Fontana

The Silk Moth Cannot Fly   88
Joanne Ruppin

The Lost Man   92
Frank Leggett

I'm glad you asked me that Owen Bullock	98
And Cyrus Wept When He Beheld Babylon Peter Ramm	100
Vase Joe Dolce	106
Ephemera Audrey Molloy	107
Sticks 'N' Stones Tug Dumbly	110
The Letter Carrier Jo Gardiner	113
On the Pre-Socratics: Thales versus Heraclitus Luke Fischer	116
The Boy From The War Veterans' Home Martin Langford	120
Facing the Obelisk / Locals / Twelve Bars Blue / Chin-Chin / Drinks Ian Crittenden	123
Remembering Iraklion Ross Gillett	130
Staying home Caroline Williamson	135
Woman is the Cow of the World Maria Vouis	138
Dust Damen O'Brien	140
Dry as a Pom's Towel Tug Dumbly	144
The Babel of Rites John Foulcher	146
Squall Anthony Lawrence	151
Colasion Ian Crittenden	155

Winner 2020 Newcastle Poetry Prize
Measures of Truth
Damen O'Brien

1. *The Cold Hard Truth*

We have been pulling hairs of ice out of
Antarctica's thousand-year frozen pelt
for the sake of the world's contested forensics.
Pulling out a white frost thorn, milky,
compact, and hard as an age of poison.

The Romans, warming their fingers at
the great forges of Tuscany and Brittany
while a vicious winter hissed on the coals
and dusted them with snow, are found in
a haze of iron, rusting the core of ice.

Nothing is ever hidden from the Earth, it
is incised, intaglio'd in some far corner,
pressed like old music in the tar of memory,
ashed like fingerprints, and folded away for
a rainy day, a century of rainy days and floods.

Disgruntled wives dosing their husbands' dinners.
Russian spies ticking and sallow with polonium.
It's all in the chemistries caught in a hair. No one
gets away with murder. Spun in misty centrifuges
we pull out cold witnesses from the core of snow.

The truth is always hardest to believe, though
the black coke marbles each spear of blue ice,
though the sea salts a rime to the top paddock, and
the virgin ice-cores stained with 400 years of smog,
sleep in university labs, cowled like a morgue.

2. The Statute of Limitations

To be honest, he blurted it out too late. He told
the birds, who told the wind who told the trees
but none of them could act, or care, and so the world
did not know to end, or his wife to leave him or
his children abandon him, for his gust of secrets.

To be honest, the statute of limitations had
always applied and his fear of getting old and
losing the careful grip on his tongue, or that the
lock on his throat would dissolve with dementia,
reached the sunset clause. Loose lips sink ships.

To be honest, all the dams burst in his head
and he muttered to the stars and he shouted at the
bedpan and he mumbled to his nurses and he gushed
and spilled with knowledge. So they raised his medication.
There was no one left to know his truth from fiction.

To be honest, he'd held the lie so long against disclosure,
his words a cyanide pill, a loved and hated truth, that
he alone could understand its value, could speak of history
like it was fresh, like the dust had not covered it long ago,
like the wound had not melted back into his skin.

To be honest, why he ever kept his secret, like
a locket or a keepsake, was lost with all his memories,
all the reasons and any chance for forgiveness.
Like the cruelty of old Greek gods, age took away
his many truths and gave him back his one lived lie.

3. *Drunk Spiders*

Getting a spider drunk like it's on a date, dropping
a tablet fizzing to the bottom of its drink, or offering
it something harder – it's the spider's first time on cocaine
and it needs a safe place to come down. Brewing it
up a black, worried that you have ruined it for art.

But it skeins and spools things in its dervish:
disjointed shard-webs; obsessive geometries, slow
spiritual spirals which trail into nothing, and
it could not have done those sober. It needs the
chemical muse, to make art no spider can make.

Juiced up flies, and suddenly the spider can do
anything, take on anything, net the world's bug,
gantry and scaffold the coruscating stars. Correlation
and deviation are at the heart of science and
the news is in: every spider creates the same drunken art.

The probative value in dealing drugs to a spider,
being an arachnid's enabler, is finite. The spider
in a man's head makes wild tears of webs and
poor art. How much of any intoxicating work is spun
from the heart, how much is slipped into our drinks?

Coleridge, Baudelaire and Burroughs, emptying
their heady vein of words, made skeins and patterns
of their lines, but how much was the drug, how much
genius? The distance between each arc and spoke is
a function of the dose. Anything can be measured.

4. *The Truth Will Make You Free*

A planet is the only test-tube that we possess,
large enough and wide enough and old enough
to encompass the truth. An epochal survey, the
sample size broad enough to be conclusive.
All the rest is randomness and bloody afterbirth.

We will know when we know, when the silt lies
down long enough to make a fossil. That
will be sufficient time to sweep away all the
Fake News. But the results are not yet in and initial
outcomes could be errors, fluctuations in the data.

When we were still many years from the results,
we put our women out of sight: our daughters
and our wives, too full of grief, too headstrong,
too open with their thoughts, too poor to pay,
imprisoned for their lives in the experiment of doubt.

Down at the Planck Length, everything is grey,
momentary and provisional, universes form and
reform like bubbles on a beach, all of it explainable
away, the observer pulling the tablecloth out from under
the observed, the magician keeping doves inside his coat.

That is why we took our wayward daughters and
our sharp-tongued wives from their homes, placed them
in asylums, named them mad. It took so long to realise
we were wrong. We did not have sufficient evidence.
We needed facts as long as life, as large, as sure as time.

5. Bone Music

It will keep surprising you, this universe, its infinite
humour: storms striating the edges of the galaxy,
and at the still centre, a supermassive black hole
sleeping with a full belly, crumbs on its sleeves,
the burning field of stars laid out like a tablecloth.

Khrushchev walled rock and roll out of Russia,
the radios tattooed Tchaikovsky into listeners eardrums
and records were melted into roads. Prokofiev and
Shostakovich were prescribed by the Soviets and
played to the packed concert halls of the damned.

But the banned music of the West was a Strange Attractor
so Russians scrambled through the backdoor bins
of clinics and hospitals searching for x-ray waste
to etch a record over the ghost of a mandible.
Hip negative ilium. They called it Bone Music.

People will die for the notes of 12 Bar Blues,
for the same reason that people will kill for it,
because it exerts a gravity of its own. When a girl band
protests in a church, or Tibetan musicians are beaten
in prison, something like echoes of drums ripples out.

Nothing is ever truly hidden, not even the silent
refuge of a supermassive black hole, found by sensors
spraying out an x-ray signal across the ordered
marches and triumphal patriotism of space. A little
pulse of sound, not unlike the music in each bone.

*Hunter Writers Centre
wishes to acknowledge the ongoing
commitment of the
University of Newcastle in providing the
Newcastle Poetry Prize*

2nd Prize
Keepers
Anthony Lawrence

When the fires
    had moved on
        to merge
with other fires
    volunteers
        & the children
of keepers
    were sent ahead
        into blacked-out
auditoriums
    of coachwood
        & hoop-pine
where grey rags
    of smoke
        still trailed
from the charred
    upper reaches
        all hives were
outlined in ash
    a single bee
        entered a hand-
span of sun
    & hovered there
        like the white
spot of a laser
    shivering over
        evidence
of lightning strike
    arson
        a downed
power line
    black-snaking
        through leaves
into flame
    as the keepers
        arrived without

nets or smokers
    the terms *apiarist*
        & *business*
were made
    redundant like raw
        honey in a spill
of engine oil
    like the word *fun*
        slipped into
a sentence about
    working conditions
        in abattoirs
interaction
    & interference
        are cut from
similar cloth
    & are not passive
        the hole
in a rain forest
    canopy light
        enters to kill
a rich groundswell
    of humus
        the heavy metal
soundtrack
    of chainsaws
        a grass-fire
quick as a mob
    of quarter horses
        cresting a rise
what these first
    responders heard
        from the trees
& the ranges
    became far more
        than the cries
and calls of dying
    birds & animals
        one volunteer

said the sound
    had left her
        with a hurt
she could feel
    in her cells
        a keeper's
daughter leaned
    on him before
        the immensity
of the absence
    of forest & as
        they turned
back into their lives
    a pair of cockatoos
        that had left
fledglings
    in a hollow
        returned to circle
over the tree
    or where the tree
        had been
the dawn chorus
    was now a field
        recording
of wings beating
    away into
        near-darkness
at two pm
    as day & night
        were skinned
& scaled replicas
    of each other
        & the echo-
locating wheel
    and flap of flying
        foxes in latex
overnight travel
    body-bags became
        crash-landings

                their pups ejected
                        or heat-welded
                                to their skin
        somewhere
                a kangaroo
                        swerved
        in a swift circular
                line to the right
                        because of fire
        somewhere
                else a kangaroo
                        swerved
        in a swift circular
                line to the left
                        because of fire

The last twelve lines have a tap-root in Earthy Anecdotes by Wallace Stevens

3rd Prize
The Long Jetty Ghazals
Robert Edmonds

I

Evening. A man in a singlet trudges straight to his shining ute.
Since seven in his service station, he's sold two litres of milk.

Morning. I'm striding briskly down a long, wide, south-bound street.
An elderly man on his patio raises his coffee to me.

At midday the lake is low and flat, frisbee deep to the mountains.
I walk the longest jetty I can, 'til the silence has me surrounded.

Why settle in a corridor, between the beach and lake?
In life, we find ourselves here, by intention or mistake.

We wheel our bins to the kerb at night beneath dull, remaindered stars.
Where paperbarks bloomed for a thousand years we've planted buffalo grass.

Our history's stuck to the toilet block. Where else would it be seen?
Outside you might be Australian. Inside European.

No mate, says John in the post office, nothing for you my friend.
Just Teen Vogue for your daughter. John! You're on the cover again!

II

Shadowy each evening, in the street they named for her,
Elsie's ghost glares at her guests – they're still her guests, she's sure.

The older European man sits at the beach with his wife,
on the rocks to watch each sun rise like the last one in his life.

Swadling haunts the lake at noon. Not going anywhere.
His ferry isn't coming and his jetty isn't there.

Above the bays and beaches, they watch us from the borders,
Norfolk pines like angels, so familiar they're unnoticed.

No moon. On the lake there's a lantern. How singular are these times.
Only one person prawning. Tens of thousands at home inside.

On the dunes I notice an octopus. Buried to the beak.
Tentacles seized by the hardened sand. Big eyes blazing at me.

Another letter for you, mate! But the handwriting's a mess.
All my friends are rejects, John. Stamped and self-addressed.

III

A girl of the Wannangine. Let's call her Turandory.
At the mouth of the Wyong River, bound for Yerrin (now Long Jetty).

Turandory rows alone. Black swans cover the water.
Black girls and women in bark canoes, mothers and their daughters.

Eyes ringed white in mourning, Turandory sees
a peaceful place for camping. Yerrin. Beach beneath the trees.

Girls and women from different tribes pull their boats up on the sand.
Some of them missing part of the smallest finger on their left hands.

Turandory fears her fate. Believes all that she has heard.
Alone on the beach beside the lake, except for a little bird.

The bird cheers Turandory. Wags its tail and sings as though
it has a message from her mother. Life is more than what you know.

Turandory's auntie smiles. Only women here, no men.
Here, you'll learn our secrets. Here, you'll find your strength.

IV

Last Sunday morning, finally (the jetty like an altar),
I saw the black swans back again. At ease upon the water.

My daughter started running. In the evenings, by the lake.
It gets me through the HSC. Yes Dad! I feel safe.

Willie Wagtail, omen bird, to the Irish and Chinese.
Djididjidi, by the lake, chipping at me from the trees.

I saw two possums on the path, and a frogmouth perch on a sign,
then a fox strode across at the roundabout, my measure in his eyes.

By day, an ancient strip of land between the sea and lake.
Beneath, at night, a spray of stars between two depths of space.

She carried her baby to safety, then lost her life to frostbite.
But Turandory's daughter lived and grew to be a midwife.

I saw possums, John, in Elsiemer Street. Rolling 'round in a game.
Before dawn, mate? Here's your stamps. And listen. They weren't playing!

V

Willemarin, clever man, speared Phillip at Broken Bay.
The smallpox outbreak started there. The natives ran this way.

Sixty-five Australians left alive on the coastal plain.
The land was counted empty and granted to Willoughby Bean.

Bean was the judge and census taker. Even in 1810
our rulers were choosing bean counters to manage the lives of men.

Billy, "last of the full bloods", drowned in the lake below.
But native Australians are everywhere, and their hearts are just as full.

It dawns on me there's some still here. One in a south-bound street.
The old man standing on his porch, raising his coffee to me.

How little we know of our landscape. How little of anything.
I thought I lived in a suburb nothing had ever happened in.

What's that on your shoulder, John? Some kind of rhipidura?
My logo, mate. The messenger bird. Sayin' somethin' to ya?

Commended
The Light We Convert
Alex Skovron

'There are only twelve notes. You must treat them carefully.'
(Paul Hindemith)

I *Prologue*

He complains his concentration grows worse.
—'Whatever I think, I'm thinking something else.'

He will not trust the night to comfort him.
—'When at last I fall asleep, it's only a dream.'

He purchases his misadventures on credit.
—'I'm frequently sorry, yet I seldom regret it.'

He wields his theology like a ringmaster's whip.
—'If a passage should rankle, I refigure it.'

He says it's the gods should be seeking asylum.
—'The gods are culpable, but who can blame them?'

He won't permit his epistemologies to show.
—'I do not know … If I knew, I'd know.'

II

Evenings are not to be trusted, each new morning
clears the mist exposed by retreating night.

Nor can you trust the night to comfort you—
whatever sleep encloses, day reopens it
with digital precision, rescored, remastered,

and all at once the music's playing faster,
redarkening the room. They say it's often said
that dreams reveal what we already knew;
that what we *think* we know, claiming the light,

lies to us. We sense miscomprehension dawning.
We blame the gods for leading us astray,
find solace in the stained-glass shards of day.

III

'My symphony is long and not exactly amiable.' (Brahms)

The crimson cleric, the congenial papa,
the marbled master, his temper never on edge,
the billiard-boy, and that fiery fist-shaker—

just several of the shades to whom I credit
my misadventures in Euterpe's realm.
I am a *fabbro* failed—
will my symphony ever see the light?

He dubs me apostle of music, while the gods
grin as I spar with the demon of my notes,
one eye on the future, the other fixated
on that stern jury. And to complicate life,
I'm hopelessly in love with my mentor's wife.

IV

There aren't too many things that I regret—
too little water under too few bridges,
the languages I'll never tell a joke in,
the times I knew I knew, yet acted else.

Not that I feel a need to apologize, mind you,
nor that the anecdotes I told seemed
inartistic, or that I harboured thinkings
dark or dangerous. No—just your random
lucky-dip of guilts I'd confess to confessing.

And in case you think I think you think I'm
a culprit, I remind you—only my art matters.
And art's a gift for which you don't apologize.

V

'I shall create a new world for myself.' (Chopin)

His precise contemporary from the east
has taken off and is living on that island
with his woman who is a man who is a woman;
how can he concentrate, with all those olive trees,
crusader churches, mosques—and then her?

Such a romantic! And yes, they call him poet
whenever he deigns to extemporize his skills;
but they say his other almost exact confrère,
that would-be Franciscan with vertiginous fingers,
is also her lover! Bully for him, I say;
but I wish I had a tenth of their dazzling talent
as I wrestle with this wretched oratorio.

VI

'Your epistemology's showing again …'
We tell her this deliberately to provoke her.
She preaches in our local Speakers' Alley,
trying to convince whoever's there, in vain,
how drink and dissolution choked her—
strangled her operatic voice. Well, her tally,

she brags, is impressive. Dozens converted
by her troubadour rhetoric, diverted

from 'meretricious haunts'—well, la-di-da!
(I must look up what epistemology means.)
We don't *know* what she knows—she seems
so much her own fantasy, with guitar.

VII

'I am a different kind of organism ...' (Wagner)

The gossips ceremoniously proclaim
such love is sure to be the death of them—
illicit offspring of a magician, with that conjuror
of palaces in clouds, every stratagem
an insurrection to shake the concert-hall.
A generation younger, can she maintain
her mission as his muse, or must she fall

to a second loveless union? And he struts
about the city, puffed with ambition, sorcerer,
a brilliant bigot lunging for the flame
of immortality. Even N shuts his door to him
now. Yet music will never be the same.

VIII

Well, our Don at the very least was spared
the ravages of conscience in old age:
those three-and-thousand conquests he shared
with his capacious ego grew into a cage
for *les tous deux*, a prison *he'd* prepared,
and when the trapdoor opened, left-downstage,
and he peered into the chasm, and was falling,
he heard a voice he recognized too late, still calling.

We toil away, trusting our songs survive
their falser notes, and our own antiphonal state.
Not each of us can be a saintly scribe—
the passions from our pages must sing our fate.

IX

*'... music which fills the soul with a thousand things
better than words.'* (Mendelssohn)

Three centuries to the year, and to the year,
between you and red Harry, who quilled as well
(they say) his clutch of wordless songs.
While, on this side of time, you pipped
your large contemporaries by a dozen months,
and your most acrid critic by near forty-eight.
You and your too-shadowed sibling,
three summers older, made a splendid comet

with a double tail. Racing the harder, she burned free
first—robbing you, both, of the wretched irony
of a *Ring* you planned that now would never be.

X

With cathedral reverence I try to control
what I am thinking as I watch her play.
No, only the music, I command myself—
and I close my eyes to no longer see her.
Is she oblivious, can she be unknowing
of my distractedness? This trite bagatelle
slipping her fingers just sweetens my torment.
Is there a physick that could calm this fever?
I struggle to listen, she finishes, closes
the keyboard and turns and then pauses.

And says: 'Focus on those scales until they flow.
Your wrists will loosen, your control will grow.'

XI

'Only when the form grows clear to you, will the spirit become so too.' (Schumann)

So what of mornings—can they be better trusted
than evening or night? Can we be sure
what the new day exposes with kindly clarity
is not simply a manner of retreating
from what we know, deep in a subterranean
cavern, deeper than any nightmare, any dream?
Are all our fears and fabrications what they seem?
And what propels that vulnerable and vain
compulsion to create, construct, compose our fleeting
tilt at cathedrals, sunken or becalmed; the alacrity
of our stubborn will to build what we think is true?
I do not know—only that time is brief, and we must trust it.

XII *Coda*

Just as these lines have led a path less clear
than camouflaged, where rhyme and reason play
their guessing-game, where hints and twists appear,

a sixfold catechism having paved the way;
so the regrets we claim, the light that we convert
to knowledge, the dark to ambiguous day,

combine (if we are so inclined) to reassert
themselves in the song we compose. I chose a brace
of years from a slice of time, strove to insert

some threads conjoining them. But any place
and any art would do, and any year.
Are not the dreams we fashion, the dreams we chase?

Commended
Groupie Acapella
Julie Manning

'In the end, we all become stories' Margaret Atwood

       I'm recalling photos of my idol
       the worn epiphanies
            or depositions - his hand

       on my shoulder beneath lips
       like-landing-strips,
            Flanders poppy mouth

       a *Sticky Fingers* decal, flashbulb
       smile & a spray-on waterfall
            of ringlets. Skank.

       Rank Arena hyena. Hip flask
       gleam in a hopped-up Cortina.
            Suburban boys in corduroy.

       Miller shirts & surfie jargon
       not my thing - I've always been
            into tragic magic, an ingenue

       in short shorts, vintage scarves
       of crepe-de-chine, bandeau top
            as decorative bra -

       a pinup doll the word *lascivious*
       was made for.
            The insides of my wrists

       are white & powder-clean, like linen
       I'd nick for handkerchiefs,
            bummed-out on

       adult conversation, hungry
       for excitement at the bleeding edge
            of groupie adulation

& my hot-spot dream: lining up
for interviews in fangirl magazines.
   We used to scout

the Strip for stars. I'd bite down
to roil my tongue-tie,
   & swallow fear, my lips

bruised with velvet plum.
I made myself flounce and glimmer:
   sure, it was fakery's strut -

shadow like a stilted bird
trailing boa-feathers in a comic
   silhouette, knee-high boots

with five-inch lifts, a shimmy
tube-top paired with costume
   gems & *Glomesh* kit.

Social rites were different then,
baby-o - we were a product
   of free love: one hundred

ways to give consent, including 'no'.
I wanted hyperdrive, mythmakers,
   the genius bad boys

my mother warned about.
In snapshots, we're pictured
   in cloche hats with netted veils,

vintage scarves & boyish breasts,
hats brim-turned,
   my friends and I were pro-

vocateurs, chests thrust out,
bodies tight, crushed
   in some hitmaker's orbit.

I'm a ruby red cartoon, a stick
of sweating dynamite!
      I'd seen him feted

at the stadium, half-undone:
call-me! - open-shirted.
      I couldn't spell *mis-*

anthropy, locked in his hotel.
Spell-bound by his cane
      and fedora, I thought

he might be counterfeit:
a hologram, or moonlight
      spun on high rotation.

I didn't understand
love or power, his reputation
      uncorrupted: moths

& butterflies can't be pinned
& framed like equal
      Lepidoptera.

Band practice. His amplifier
humming like a hot-rod Roadster.
      We toured in a limo,

the birthmark on my thigh
buzzed with atom hearts,
      not mothers, his power

pack energised: not surprised,
my close friend found his bed.
      I was broken-hearted,

hurt so bad, but the song
remained playing
      & I can't go home again.

A singer with a mane is waiting
at a jet, beside the engines,
        spilling blonde space junk

& orbiting the tarmac
in his open shirt, beads & jeans –
        snake-hipped, denim-clad,

an attention span
I couldn't breathe through:
        'Pre-Raphaelite God!

Then the beer-loving muso
easily interchangeable
        a Doobie Brother, Eagle,

Black Sabbath clone, spider-web
shirt, childish, like a book
        cover at home

a ruddy heartbeat wearing
an artillery belt, death-wish
        star in a boudoir

with a fireplace and jet engine
flanked by amplifying skin
        and a brass gong

like a schooner -
completing his equipment.
        Or another like quick-

silver in incognito shadow
named after some
        rugged movie scene hero.

Slightly dull but talkative
& card-carrying ordinary,
        though shirtless

at his keyboard, he made it
to the turnpike
      cloaked in anonymity.

I was the muse with glitter
crusted lashes, bewitched
      in teenage makeup, our names

etched into conquest diaries,
& no one checked ID's.
      The one I was be-

sotted with, the one astride
a twin-neck, returned
      with his girlfriend

but she's older than he was
when he had me and had me.
      Her ringlets look familiar,

her need an open highway.
I watch myself like
      I'd watch a movie trailer.

I keep the photo's in a cellar
infused with Revlon *Charlie*.
      I keep the riffs locked

tight like a box of maniacs.
There's one snapshot
      of my mother, smouldering

in a lurex pullover, at a concert
with her arm like a steering
      wheel lock around a star.

I see her pick her way through alleys,
home from fringe cafés,
    an elongated shadow

past the drive-by. I know her daughter
was in trouble: she moved out when
    the limo stopped arriving.

box of maniacs from 'The Arrival of the Bee Box', Sylvia Plath
one hundred ways to give consent including 'no' from 'The Encyclopedia of Trouble and Spaciousness'
Rebecca Solnit, 2014.

Hunter Writers Centre Award
the bees
Christopher (Kit) Kelen

up

to hive the mazed wood
because a forest lost us
afoot, where no leaf falls

fresh green to twig

all on the wing and never a prayer
store summer from the flowers spilt
breathe the secret paths of air

in ways of season got beyond

hear rain from distance
and see it to the pond, this age
of spears stood lightly thrown

fresh on the face where fallen

it has our hills away
climbing to be forgotten
a flutter — can you come consider?

rise with an inch up sun

in among leaves, bright
to be all other-worlded here
their pollen to the clock waxed hands

I bring a magic door — see me

and paint the sunshone world for you
so crooked woods bend paths
and these new pages of the tree

were such a song

stood past the map
sweet summer in the branches yet
last bee in its dusk flight and vanish

having never been before

the track is not where it was

winds twisting out of recollection

someone is under, for a spell
and all around my wonder

let the scourge be sweet

names of the bees, shall we recite?

no, they are secret still

bees

spin like sparks

in their night of smoke, hoard the sun

they wear it in stripes, wear the dark

in the hour before the shadows come, still golden

bees have gathered the day to this end
the light within the hive

telling them

secrets intimate, births, marriages
the goings and the comings home

but most of course the keeper's death

like a rosary each blessing

they are of an afterworld, from
and through the mirror

knock on the hive and tell the tune
lift the lid, lean in

the bees must all be told

an Easter of their passion

call then the colour of lions

finding, getting   bearing about

a winter of their warming

can you hear how they tell?

who will box the flight?
in leaf such a sky as they bring

woken, are the drift of toil to joy

see question marks for halo round

call us to other hidden things

in the dance we never see
bees are teaching again

they are calligraphers of heaven

with tracks of pointed fire, scribes set down the day

may we be minded, arc and tangent, climb empyrean,
melt wings to wax — no two turns same

show the moment for itself

such signatures they make away
we follow to find ourselves

the bees are a wheel

whoever worked the treetops
saw the unleafed sun
and knew the honeyed roundness

or else we might have dreamt
our flight among the flowers
flitting one to one

a hover and a hum

over the hay
on the threshing floor

how brief a flower, all?

bees live in a poem like this

sunstriped through shutters
a whiff away low, over the chaff

guess at the angle, gyre and climb

bees are an innocence passing

told always on alive, a hum

to the sugar in the bowl

in this afternoon, to tea

the workers

could be queen, each

because they went their Monday rounds
and made their ways where no bee was

out of the hive night nameless
who make pure the light

here they are far in the firstness again
and petal bound to tell the deeps
one and one more they bring

that is so the flower sings
that never was before

the hive is a store of labour

a system of shadows
take off and landing

endlessly from hollow rock
rank and file swarming

all golden, by the book
fates are offered, wheat kneaded with

and where they hive
it's honey cakes for Cerberus

bind a cup with wreaths around

before Dionysus took wine
there was this libation

the elocution of the bees

tell on, and sweetly once bees spoke

before that though sang valour, loves

the bee-loud grove, the bean rows
hung in heads, alley long the roses

no honeyed words but hard fought
precious we are to hearts

how we are the tribe we are
we were so we will be

seasons are in the bees

the summer hive on fire
dog days camp outside
all angered as one insect, we

drowsy, dodge a raindrop

and if the winter queen should lay
then all of us may die

the spaceman and the smoking gun

here home in memory – the mindspeck
more than one star's light shows

as pictured in the compound eye?
bringers of sunshine so, aliens among

all godlight in the littlest

door in the hive, figure moted in smoke

how far such craft are come!

make a hole in the page

who flies through?

the watercolour bees, those in oil, the macro

the wings are faster than the eye, and make a garden where they go

bees of the dream imagine us hived in the honey and no one at home

of tinsel lit, here are the angels unbibled

sting my enemy and die
I go to grace that way

come to the flower and kiss like this
keep it under your wings

time in the text

where the bees have gone, all are immortal

and best never knowing which way we are
how we came or where to go

the bees were a suitcase I set up
not wanted on the voyage

now in a cowslip's bell I lie
you see the arrows after flight?

nun scribblers in their little cells
with all the words that ever were

they are making truth of light
that you may read it here

jolly bees all vanish into a book

prophetic till the last I think it is the holy madness

(satyrs clash cymbals, chase into a tree)

was a time this was the sweetest thing…

stone from the bounds of ocean creviced

    ambrosia is brought
they're drunk on one or another
through dust, through weight of day, heroic

a book like this one you too are in   and will we
come out ever at all to give the breeze its wings?

a wilderness wild guess towards
the place does not consist of hours

we follow other creatures to the forest in the garden

growl, flap, do the business, tear

no one has understood yet why is this crisis to be?

bees bring us to an oracle — they have the power of rain

abuzz

and even before the speaking sun
    from nectar to proffer

with just a little meaning jig
    lift from these waters, fly

the god of all is a visiting bee

a poppy bruised, meadow me
        lay acres between

rye and the spring — all this propitious

stole, was stung and stings too

at the dripping comb — come lap

down

    flit errant in amber arrested   in a pond reflect
    shone through the skin, for a mirror, look in

    bumble and drone — a little bounce, buffet

    see through the smoke till devil may
    driven from time altogether, banking…

    all our sweetness and all, often dimmed to riff
    a kind of doom must be

    in wings of where we trick the light
    come at it out of the blue
    to feed upon mere air

**HUNTER
WRITERS
CENTRE**

*Hunter Writers Centre,
an incorporated association since 1998, administers
the Newcastle Poetry Prize
for the University of Newcastle.
The centre is the peak literary organisation of the
Hunter Region, New South Wales, Australia.
hunterwriterscentre.org*

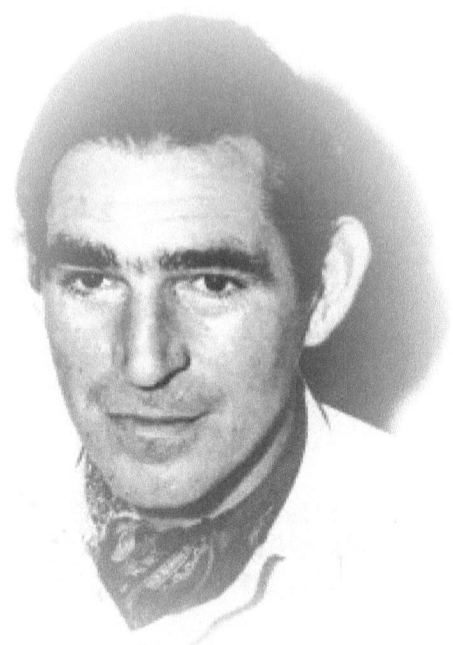

About the Harri Jones Memorial Prize

Thomas Henry (Harri) Jones was born in a remote area of Wales in 1921, the eldest of five children and the only son in a poor rural family. He won scholarships to secondary school in Builth Wells and then to university in Aberystwyth. His studies were interrupted by World War II when he served in the Navy. He met his wife, Madeleine, when they were demobbed after the war. After completing his Master's degree in the post-war years, he taught English to returned servicemen at the Naval Dockyards in Portsmouth, England. He and Madeleine moved to Newcastle NSW in 1959 with their three young daughters. Harri had obtained a lectureship in the Department of English of the then University College of Newcastle, an offshoot of the University of New South Wales. This was meant to be a short-term move, with the hope of returning to Britain when Harri secured a lectureship there.

Harri is a well-known Anglo-Welsh poet and in addition to his books of poetry he is well represented in anthologies of poetry in Australia and elsewhere. He published his first volume of poetry in 1957. His fourth and last was published posthumously in 1966. He was very well regarded as a lecturer despite the alcoholism that marred his latter years and ended with his untimely death by drowning in 1965 at the age of 43. After his death, family and friends donated money in his memory to set up a poetry prize to continue in perpetuity.

Harri Jones Memorial Prize
Rock Hopping
Peter Ramm

> *It's what we forget that defines us, and stays in the same place,*
> *And waits to be rediscovered... Someday I'll find it out*
> *And enter my old outline as though for the first time.*
> — **Charles Wright**

I

                  The rocks erupt before us like pumice
Teeth on the milky sands of Jervis Bay
       —Lined and pitted like the tidal fissures
              Of Currarong Creek. We skip and bramble
      Our buckets, brimming with tackle; spinners,

                Sinkers and hand stretched line clatter and clunk.
Mother maps a path between the shallow pools
      Packed with Neptune's pearls, and black sheoaks
            Peer over her shoulder. We're adrift furlongs
    From father who's rigged and casting for bream.

              In our esky pilchards and pipis
Slosh in midday and leach their watercolours,
      Burley churns the water, and whiting dart
           Like quivering silver arrows—the way
    Death lures the living, one beat at a time.

             I always loved spotting for crabs, hearing
Them chitter beneath the cyclopean
      Boulders like tap dancers with poor timing.
           Sometimes we'd catch one awash in the shallows
    And drop them before they pinched our fingers—

            Later, a man would teach me to bait
Grouper by quartering their carapace.
      But now, rock canyons form a fortress
           From the wind who's whipped the waves to white
    And the seagrass meadows into obeisance.

                        An eastern reef egret watches—elderly
And wise as we pluck limpets from mermaid
            Inlets, foraging through memories.
                        He lifts off, fades to the charcoal headland,
            And I've begun to leave pieces of myself

                        Forgotten like shells scattered on the foreshore.
Sand bites at our shins, and in time's swell
            The line to father is snagged on oysters;
                        Now I'm barely here, hopping sandstone
            In a race against the tide lapping his shoes.

II
                        After twenty years, the gannet's suntanned
Heads still torpedo the sea like flaming darts,
            The grains of technicolour sand still bleach white,
                        And my son's hand is cemented in mine.
            I've measured the stride he needs to take

                        Over slits and slips in the rocks—an abyss
To him. I know how barnacles can curse your knees,
            Why we wrap our soles with silicon.
                        He stops to poke at periwinkles
            And purple urchins, their newness beams

                        In his eyes. Now, I carry his grandfather's
Cork handled rod, drawn and taut, its hook
            Looped back through the guides. The sheoaks still sway
                        In westerlies, but the bream are less now.
            Seaweed mounds ferment the dunes, squelch under foot,

                        And run in tea stained rivulets down the berm.
I've brought him to the promontory I've fished
            In recollection, to wet the long line
                        Of remembrance—to my mother's words
            And the patchworked freckles of my father's hands.

                        But the boy finds his way to the beach;
He plunders the sand like my present
            And finds treasure in this day. A family
                        Of black cockatoos nests in the hollow
            Of a spotted gum, the hatchlings a rasping

      Choir in discord—beckoning their father
Back from his palatine arc overhead.
    I meander down. Finn's feet are deep
      To his ankles in backwash, and he fumbles
Through the ocean's jealous undertow.

      In the white-water each piece of sea floor
Is refracted, an everchanging
    Geology of what was and what could be;
      My son plunges hands into the foam
And in his shirt he hauls a fistful of shells.

Local Award
The Ways You Haven't Left Me
Judy Johnson

1.

In the stroke ward, after the bilateral fireworks went off in your head
your stare didn't leave me. You were at the end of your rope
like that bucket that kept descending into the deepest well of us
then dragging up water in your eyes. I heard the insistent clang
of something galvanised banging against a tunnel of walls. Or maybe
just the medicine trolley doing its rounds. But suddenly I knew
what you would have me do. A dozen times I rehearsed drawing
the pale curtain around the disapproving tongue-clicks of its circular
rail then like some half-rate magician with budget props, making you
disappear. And afterwards, removing to the bedside table the stuff of
soft violence wrapped in its pillowcase of mercy, before opening the
curtains again. But I couldn't do it. Instead I read aloud from your love
poems to me, shamelessly using your own lines to tether you to earth a
little longer.

My love is a softly opened season. She has laugh lines on her knuckles.

2.

You thought you had time to plan your exit. Like Jack Gilbert
you wanted to be torn apart by tigers not nibbled to death
by the mice of your Dementia. The closest thing to jungle cats
in our town were the coal trains: Arcadian boars rumbling a warning
from a suburb away then closer, two diesel-yellow eyes burning holes
in the night. The wheels would squeal on the rails to sharpen
your mind on their whetstone. Letting you know in your last moments
you were fully alive. But the thought wouldn't leave you: the yawning
driver near the end of his shift. In the console lights, his future face
dappled with flashbacks of psychotropic red. And that soundtrack
like low pitched smacks of bread dough in the mixer when it's thrown
around by the kneading hook. Your body thumping under his feet
in the cab before the dead-man's brake kicked in.

Night burns like a candle in a shrine without a god.

3.

You have missed the last train to anywhere except this nursing home. Your peering is red-rimmed like a seagull's, fixed on a point above my right shoulder. It seems your one last task is as figurehead on a sinking ship. The Captain and his higher executive crew have taken the lifeboats and deserted you. But the oldest retainers still keep the engines going while your hull sinks lower every day and your body lists to starboard unless someone props you up. These stayers have the names of Shakespearean witches: hypothalamus, amygdala, hippocampus. I wish chanting their many syllables could stir up a spell to counteract our curse. The Italians would say you've lost your *Sprezzatura*. The nonchalance to conceal the difficult art of life. It is all too visible now, how hard you struggle to get out of a chair, to hold your bladder and bowels. To walk the few steps from the door to your bed. I fuss with the buttons on your cardigan, inspect your nails. Kiss the tops of your bruised hands from where the blood thinners have made of your skin, a series of ink blots on fragile paper. But all the while I am so calm and tender, inside my chest the panic flutters. The wild bird of my love for you is locked in this cage of futile gestures. I'm amazed you can't feel its trembling body striking the bars.

Skin is free. You pay for your scars.

4.

A carer brings crushed pills in chocolate syrup. When you open your mouth for the spoon, a line of lip-spittle stretches and snaps. When you yawn I see another shard of filling has broken off from one of your molars. But there will be no dentist unless you are in pain. You've gained some kilos. Even though the means by which your favourite foods (jelly and custard, cake and ice cream) reach your taste buds has been outsourced to professional strangers.
I am glad you have some extra ballast. One day soon you'll forget how to swallow. Already you chew too long as though anything more than a strand is a log that must be shifted around the conveyor belt of your tongue then milled into dust or pap by the cross-cut saw of your teeth before it can move on. Purees will be next, then Sustagen. Your doctor will suggest a feeding tube, which I'll refuse.

The sky burns black past each event horizon.

5.

The towel I wrap around your unresisting shoulders keeps slipping and I think a peg I could have brought from home might have held the edges together. I stand behind you and the room fills with buzzing. Such an intimacy to do this, touch the warm contours of your skull. When the harvesting's done, I run a palm over the stubbled field thinking of mice scattering and hawks going down slowly in circular spirals some invisible drain in the sky. I massage those patches behind both ears phrenologists chart as the place of conjugal affection. I hope the hair clippers like the probe of an ultrasound have brought into focus my shadow. If I find the right pressure point will you remember my name?

Your skin has rubbed me into dreams.

You held back that first night we made love. Your initial touch free of coercion. Cupped hands gathered my then-long hair above my head into a nest of tinder. It was my decision to throw in the glowing coal and set us both alight.

We pad to the bedroom to write a long, long poem on each others bodies.

I have an answer for Neruda. Here is one thing sadder than a train standing in the rain: the demeaning squeak of a plastic mattress-protector on the single bed of a once-proud man as he is tucked in tight to the size of his diminishment. I lie next to you. Put my ear to your chest to listen to your heart's game of hopscotch. Three beats with a quick pause to pick up the stone then a double landing at the end, two feet hitting the ground a millisecond apart before turning to do it all again.

6.

You said they were Frankenstein bolts you'd unscrewed from both sides of your neck. They looked to me as though they'd come from Bunnings. But I accepted them as an allegory of trust, never knowing exactly what you mean't. Just that you thought you were made from the corpses of two failed marriages. And you'd had to stitch yourself back into the resemblance of a man, for me.

She is domains of joy around walls of old terror.

I sit in the car outside the nursing home. The breeze is fussing around the bracts of old ladies in the branches of the crepe myrtle. They wave me goodbye with their pink tissues. But I can't move, feeling the monstrous attention of those bolts burrowing into my ribs. It hurts so much, I bend over the steering wheel and the tears come.
I remember then the breast-cancer port the size of a cigarette case that was inserted under the skin near my sister's collarbone. Even if every vein refused entry, the poisons of healing could still be pumped in.

When she cries, the sound is scissors cutting sand and the hot tinkle of broken promise.

7.

If you are anywhere now, it's in the top paddock of our garden where the sky is lower–all the tints of blue at the paint shop in an overfilled balloon–or sometimes pre-storm, the bellies of grey-shark clouds cruising under the sunlight. On violet dusks in summer we waited until the reserve a kilometre away released its catapult of bats. And at dawn when the air was a menthol chrysalis, the day waking up inside it we took binoculars and coffee to watch the mating pair of red wattle birds high in the silky oak: their squeaky ratchets, their total indifference to anything that wasn't food or a threat. We'd sit in silence on the bench seat, with its furry doilies of lichen clinging to the slats. Rest our cups on the mossy concrete rim of that rectangle that marked the place where many years ago you buried our boy, but not before with solemn harrows did the deep work with the shovel. You threw your second-best leather jacket into the grave to keep him warm in that endless off-leash park where good dogs must surely go. We held each other and cried a little. His devotion had made us try to be worthy of it. And we were afraid that thing inside us that yearned to be better had also died with him.

And the shame burned me, to be loved like that.

8.

I dream of you every night, though sometimes you take the form
of other men. As there is less and less of you, my longing fills the
blanks with cyphers of old lovers, trying to replicate your DNA but
making mistakes in the sequencing. One day perhaps I'll only evoke
you in an elusive whiff of Old Spice on a busy street. Or you'll settle
in my throat as a partial emotion, a barely-there piece of grit rubbing
against consciousness all day. Over time resembling an un-perturbed
pearl. Until then, I pretend you haven't left me. You're just in your shed
at your whittling. The making is all, you once said. The mind
unfastened from its moorings. The body propelling the blade through
the wood like an oar. Surrounded by gougers and those expensive
Kawasei-Nori carving chisels: blue-paper steel, laminated with soft
iron, handles wrapped tightly in the grip of bamboo. You're still
searching for the gnarls and burls to find the entry point to that
essential flow.

*A good poem conjoins surprise and necessity. This it must have learned
from a kiss.*

The nursing home has rung to say you've had another fall, but you
seem unhurt. It always happens when you overbalance, bending
to touch the floor. Only I know what you're looking for as your
fingers reach down like a knife to dig a moat of bas-relief and
free the lost carving of my face from the pattern in the lino.

*You notice how hopeful her eyes are and already you owe her something
of great value.*

9.

It's winter. You're still alive. The liquidamber has shed the last of
its parchment leaves. Skim milk sun shines through the bare branches
in bicycle spokes. Our orange trees have lit up with Christmas in July
baubles. I will bring you some of the freshly-squeezed juice, lift the cup
to your lips, wipe away the pulp from your chin with a hanky.
This morning I saw a single strand of gossamer quivering with dew.
It had come loose from a web not strung tightly enough by the spider.

I am like an empty fly rope on a high trapeze still swaying though all of the spangled beauties have jumped off for good. I miss you. Some days like a limb, some nights like a torso, then only the cat witnesses how completely I can fall apart. But sometimes when I see the hint of a smile on the vacancy of your face, I wonder if after all you're in a place of warmth where bees spin sticky threads of summer. You never did like the cold, having endured for years the minus-zero months in Minnesota. Who am I to say your life's no longer worth living, just because I can't imagine what it's like. Blessed with Knausgaard's 'soothing compress of hereness', you always seem un-troubled.
As though there is only the uninjured moment. The singular prayer.

We are more than our wounds.

I don't know why, but I keep thinking about the Velveteen Rabbit in that children's story. With its shabby ears, most of its fur rubbed off and its eyes hanging by a thread. But none of that mattered because it had been made Real by being loved for a very long time. And how the Skin Horse, who was always honest, told the Velveteen Rabbit that there were some who couldn't ever believe, because they didn't know the extent of what love could do. And how it hurts sometimes to be Real, but it's worth it. And anyway, no matter what, it can't be undone.

Lines in italics are extractions from the poetry of Rob Riel.
Jack Gilbert was an American poet who died in 2012. His statement about preferring to be torn apart by tigers rather than nibbled to death by mice is from a radio interview.
Karl Ove Knausgaard is a Norwegian author. The phrase 'like a soothing compress of hereness' refers to the healing powers of the natural world.
The Velveteen Rabbit is a stuffed toy in the book of the same name by Margery Williams.

The Island in the Roundabout
Chris Andrews

It was the coveted upstairs room
at the front, with a balcony, his
by virtue of seniority.
He went in, snatching things off the floor.
In that first, unforgotten moment
the space had a pre-electric depth:
a mirror's elliptical silver
swimming in the wardrobe's charcoal bulk.
The sash window showed how a street lamp
can gather a nest of glistening twigs.
What am I doing here? she wondered.
And: Who still has that many CDs?
He hesitated, hoping to choose
something that wouldn't be too over.
What I could do with a room like this!
she thought, mentally placing her things.
In hay-fever time, elm keys would swirl
on the balcony around a cup
of slow tea and her drying toenails,
and when exams were done, the others
would go back to Bendigo or Shep
or Wang or wherever and leave her
alone, luxuriously alone.
He came and put his hands on her hips.
She wouldn't have said it was over
that music; it had always been dull.
He was dancing her unhurriedly
towards the bed. He could dance. And talk.
He had gone to the big world out there
and come back with travel capital.
But he was a questioner as well.
Maybe she'd given away too much.
Her hands had already discovered
that he wasn't as thin as he looked.
With that moustache, he reminded her
of the well-oiled conjuring artist
in an ironic remake. The sky
from where she lay was still indigo

between branches and scaffolding pipes.
An arpeggiated major chord
carried from the station. When he ripped
the shiny plastic wrapper, she balked.
Not that it all had to be sublime.
She wouldn't have said he was creepy
(though she could imagine he might be
one day), just a bit too interested
in the whole first time thing. He sat up
and said there was no hurry, at all,
looking winded and tight in the face.
Then: 'Why would you like guys, anyway?'
There's an extrapolation, she thought.
And: Funny how people will not rest
until they have a box around you.
A molecule was still there for him:
he rummaged in a drawer and began
pinching, rolling, expertly licking.
There was no denying it: she too
had the spooky power to divert
the flow of somebody else's blood.
He jerked the squealing sash up and stepped
out onto the splintery grey boards.
After a moment's hesitation
she pulled her jumper on and followed.
There was a scent of pittosporum.
He had lifted his mini blow torch
when a squad car pulled up in the street.

> Two officers in tactical pants
> approached a car parked in the lamplight.
> A tap on the window made the man
> inside look up with a fading smile
> from the book propped on the steering wheel.

Watching this scene unfold from above,
the artist conjured his joint away,
gave her shoulder a squeeze and whispered:
'Reading in a stationary vehicle:
ignorance of law is no excuse.'
The knot in his face had come undone.

A search of the reader's bag turned up
nothing but a metal box with knobs
the likes of which she had once seen deep
in the jungle of a studio.
There was only so long she could say:
Sex is something other people do.
But she had thought it often enough
to go on feeling that it would be,
that it was a kind of betrayal.

> Thumb on fob, the senior constable
> lifted her head to yawn and saw them:
> the wild-haired kids on the balcony,
> freshly disentangled, half their luck.
> The boy was smiling. The girl's hand rose
> as if to wave, then hovered and dropped.

Before her palm settled on the rail,
she saw it coming: as the squad car
glided away with submarine ease,
impeccably lubed, he turned, brows high,
head tilted, and said: 'Friend of the force?'
Maybe just then, in a way, she was
but, embarrassed, she had turned to look
at the island in the roundabout,
its three loose-limbed, lemon-scented gums
swaying almost imperceptibly.

Nudged
Rod Usher

A nudge, a tug, now slack again.
Sunrise eyes squint across water
that confirms the Earth is flat.
Nylon slacks across forefinger.

Words out here are monosyllabic:
boat, bait, bite, spike, gill, salt,
sky, swell, wait…
Reeling, a shape slowly ascends

free but caught by a dumb idea
it follows up the baitless barb,
undulating beauty entranced
by metal that would lock into lip

or be swallowed whole and rip
organs as the fine line is hauled
to thrashed drowning in dry air
or knifepoint on the scaly board.

Just on surface, the big flathead's
tiny brain or tremendous instinct
homes it down the slippery slope,
and the bare hook takes my eye.

Isolations
Paul Hetherington

1.
Her father waits on a park bench, dropping crumbs until the birds are used to him. He tries to discern complexities in their song—like torrid gustings of light. He lifts up those that come close, sensing tenderness in their bony frames and time panting. Sometimes he feels their song on his skin like a faint burring of feathers.

2.
Mud hems the house where a lawn once felted a riverfront. The real estate agent hammers a sign. Earth flakes underfoot and garden beds are spatters of bloom. She buried crockery and dolls' heads, built labyrinthine hose-fed waterways, scratched obscenities into the earth, memorialised pets with plum wood crosses. The purple fruit fell and basketfuls were made into staining, sticky jam. Now she points to a skewed stone wall and picks up a Matchbox Aston Martin. On hands and knees, she propels it at speed.

3.
The trumpeter splits Sunday morning's light. People in the square pay little heed. She's looking skyward as her pram's wheels bounce across cobbles. The southern Italian town falls higgledy-piggledy down a hill, its narrow streets like threads pulled by a needle. After a fractious night she walks to a beach where illicit cargo has long been hauled. The trumpet's notes chase her to a cave's black hole. Fishermen throw lines and speak rapidly, as if exhorting the tide. She nods, opening her hands in the trumpet's mouth, broadcast far and wide.

4.
Her mother spoke as if seizing reality—turning it over, inspecting its forms, sifting its iterations. Palpability faded even as she grasped the household cat; even as her bare feet flexed on Persian carpet. Latinate forms intruded. Yet, sunshine startled and birds shrilled *now*—the day opening into staccato exclamation, disentangled from saying. She carried herself towards the river's messy grammar, untangling nets and casting lines, dragging 'the catch' in buckets.

5.
She barely notices her body in the mirror. She buys a Portuguese salad bowl and fills it with oranges. The gifts sent by a friend don't suit the space. The apartment has a collection of raucous CDs that match her sense of exigency. She can't say what pulls and presses her; what climbs through her spine at night. She makes her way towards the city where an Enoteca supplies cheap Tempranillo and a supermarket tray holds ripe artichokes. Outside, her future continues to walk. At night she wakes, listening to the footsteps.

6.
Roof beams square the light. The back garden and cobwebbed studio squeeze towards a meadow. Her aunt sits outside, on an iron-framed chair where a rose's tendrils flicker, refusing to address her paintings, claiming her father's violence returns in memory: 'I was three years old and every day he thrashed me.' There's bamboo thrusting through lawn; broken roof shingles; stone walls prized apart. Her aunt says, 'Buy bananas, cereal and beans—and a tube of violet.'

7.
Cats adorn an exquisite garden where wind gathers a pine tree, like an embrace enfolding a child. A crane hides next to the pool where koi are as plump as languorous cats; colours rise in glades of water. She might be stone, seeing flickers of surface as the crane barely moves, shifting its head towards another pose. Each minute buries her further. Someone speaks but she can't decipher the words.

8.
A clock slows and her uncle's body weakens into a final congestion of sleep. Her sense is of something opening but she can't look at it squarely. Its hands creep across a small stand of beeches; a noise like a ratchet accompanies light. Vocalisations interrupt words. She hears a hum that might be purring light, or shadow, or a slowly failing clock. Beeches are the clock's hands shaken in a fist.

9.
In the studio's yellow haze she sees her grandfather. He doesn't look at her but something in the light's colour carries him—as if composed of dust and wood grain; as if his easy way of speaking lifts in motes and breeze. A soft force like his breath on her face; a redolence of skin rising from upholstery. Though he's disarticulated in flame, she leans into his posture.

10.
In the photograph her brother faces the river, chewing gum, fishing and standing under the brown weight of summer. She stands close and apart, occasionally leaning towards his shoulder. He shallow-dives into the water. Weeks after the image was taken he went to live with his father. She's hoped to know him since, but during visits he jams childhood into clipped phrases buried among the rise of stocks and companies—and, when leaving, merely waves. Last week he grimaced and turned his head, looking towards the eroded foreshore. She observes him there—as late afternoon presses on his skin like a damp, warm cloth, watching the pulsing frills of jellyfish, inspecting jags of driftwood, failing to see her.

Annotations
John Foulcher

Prologue

It was thoughtless, dying in December,
ruining our Christmas. Dad died in August,
which gave us time. I recall that year,
huddling in a rain-pocked festive tent
at Auntie Dulce's: the soaked ceiling,
saggy dread, slough of makeshift home,
Mum and Dulce indoors, away from us. . .
As always, Mum was more considerate,
passing in March, though she echoed
through the house at our next Christmas do,
where talk was a game of omission.
But you gave us a funeral this Advent,
became a robber St Nikolaus, stealing
the love you'd given, wrapping it in absence:
forever under the tree, that present for the future.

Nine Chapters

1

A spiteful wind is pruning the April sky -
there are leaves all over the terrace,
and the cold is taking root. I never
saw your body. It was shrinking,
tightening around your soul, as if
the soul were the marrow in our bones.
I will not see you again, though still
I see your daughters by your bed,
like leaves that settle on an April morning.

2

Never yourself at the centre of things,
you told me you didn't want the fuss
of dying. You might make it to New Year,
I said, hoping death could be a stone

skipped across calm water. *It's like
everyone's trying to say goodbye to me
but how can I say goodbye? What's me
won't be me, you know? Do you ever
get tired of the room full of people?*
You bet I do. I leaned across the bed
and embraced you forever. When the clocks
began again, you kissed my cheek, cast me off.

3

The week before, as we wandered
the corridors, a nurse had stopped us:
Brothers? I was proud of that snap,
though it was only our bones. I promise
you, I said when she'd gone, I won't
have you suffer the indignity of a poem.
Sure you said, smiling. *I'll bet you won't.*

4

When Dad died, time was up for us
and happiness. We shuffled about
the house, the rooms cluttered with
nothing. Mum wilted into our bedroom
while we spread out in the front room
she couldn't bear to be in, your bed
on one side and mine on the other.
In those years, you made sure I did
dumb things, still, as we tried to untie
grief's mess of knots. We stopped
playing the games Dad had played,
cricket and football, dreamt up our own
shoddy contests no one would lose.
Then you were gone, assuredly as Dad
but alive and elsewhere, into the arms
of a girl (we never talked of girls), lured
to a sort of rebirth. Our years alone
had been lost years, a tangle of years.
You weaved among them, and I followed.

5

Decades on, in the decade after you
gave work away, you and Jenny flew
to Paris, where I'd been practising ennui
for months. I knew Paris like my palm
and took you everywhere you wanted,
brought you home to your hotel room.
We scaled the towers of Notre Dame,
though I made sure you braved the line
for tickets, while I was French in a café.
Once, in the Louvre, I helped you
tick off Jenny's list of unmissables,
led you through the slush of tourists
to pretty, armless Venus de Milo.
While I plotted a path to *The Lacemaker*,
you stared at Venus, whispered
So that's it, as if the world were full
of almosts and not-quites. Yeah, that's
it, I said, already on the next stair.
I glanced back, saw childhood tears,
and knew how new you were to wonder.
But I was leading you then, subverting
deference, and I let you linger there,
pre-teen for the moment, in that passage
of the wretched years. At last, Venus
grew dull, Vermeer could wait no longer.
OK you said, *What's next? Let's go.*

6

When you last made a pilgrimage
to the old country church we'd snared
from the Catholics, we spent our time
smashing it up, preparing the way
for its conversion to a house.
We took down the confessional first,
that plywood box of sins, splintering it
with hammer-holes of dullish light,
extracting penance from the dust.
Next the vestibule, small sanctuary

before worship, made of firmer stuff:
clamped to the floor and braced in iron,
it swayed when the struts gave way,
then slammed into the floor, dumping
its biretta of bat-shit and dirt across the nave.
At last, the altar, clutching at holiness,
digging itself in, as we prised it up,
apart. We saw what we had done then,
and it was good. We rested, on the first day.

7

A year later, on the edge of emptiness,
you said quietly, *I think I'm going to
convert.* For thirty years, you sat with Jenny
at Mass, crossing your arms at the host. Now,
you set yourself to dive into that dark sea.
*I don't know about heaven and that,
but I want my church around me, you
know?...* When you stood before the altar,
you wore a white shirt, white as an alb.
Outside, in the lit morning, the spire rose
like a column of smoke, into a cloudless sky.

8

You were not always grave. Once,
before phones could work free of wires,
I recall how you'd sat in your car
outside our house and rung me from
the air. *I'm on my way to town. Can I visit?*
This was last century, the century of disgrace.
Sure. When will you get here? Thinking
hours. *I'll let you know.* I let go the line,
but before I'd settled the snug coupling
handset, you knocked, holding before you
that thing from the future, rudimentary
as a pencil case. The kids couldn't believe it,
they loved the way you slipped around
inside life, sneaking up on us, the way
everything was practically a joke. You made
such beautiful fools of us, over and again.

9

In the hospital dusk, you asked me
to read aloud the novel you'd started
but had lost the will to finish.
I didn't have a clue what it was about
but read as if you were a child preparing
for another night. You closed your eyes:
I was sibilant and fricative,
a dose of vowels and consonants
to help you breathe more freely,
hoping in the end those words meant
something more than sounds, half-heard
and half-recalled, as some lives tend
to be. . . Soon the pool of murky sleep,
opiate indifference, the world
beyond the window fading in the dark.

Epilogue

Dignity is a seamless,
regular beat, never lost
or given in tributes, recreations.
You were your own verse,
one among many, you'd
say, but to us particular,
like the dusk that gathered
outside your hospital room,
its azure crushed cotton
forever fading and remade
as pale sunrise, blanching
the horror of this or any night,
as if it were nothing to speak of.

Feral
James Lucas

In the Gardens by the Yarra I run into Ferdinand Mueller
sowing, in the ashes of his billy fire, blackberry seed.
He looks like Friar Lawrence but fatter.
He's telling me there are no weeds. He knows his Shakespeare
just a little. That spells danger.
This is the Victorian era in which men know better.
You see the work of his hands prosper
in ditches and on both banks of the river
berries cluster thick as turds of thicket-panicked sheep.
Mueller's eyes see this, and further, his face ripened
to the purple of his portrait postage stamp,
his packet fat with decorations from the royal houses,
fat with the seed of *genus muellerina*. His lizard's longer
than a snake. His iridescent stag beetles
are matchbox muscle cars that shimmer lime and purple
glossier than boots shone sheepshit khaki.
He spills the billy, badgers me to find his statue,
rages at the Premier, rages against white-anting
Toorak aesthetes. We promenade, walk by the ponds,
while he makes plans for planting bluegum
into Africa and North and South America
and he assures me his work will continue in the pasture
science of acclimatised legumes and grasses, cattlefeed,
in hamburger patties by *Uber*. He's gone, not gone. I find myself
within this zoo for plants. And who am I to call him vandal?

2

Voyages had their undersides,
wormy hulls hitch-hiked by shellfish,
ballast to the fox and rabbit

we'd decided would be coming to this country
in the circumstances we'd decided:
submariners, illegal immigrants and pioneers,

fore-runners to disgorgees
arriving by the harbourful when giant tankers purged
to ingest minerals that sweetened account deficits;

fore-runners to the giant wakame
mermaid tails who ate their mermaids,
to dinoflagellates who poisoned oysters.

Tim Low, walking on the shores
of D'Entrecasteaux Channel,
prised his final oyster from the rocks

and took in a free side of algae
courtesy of ballast from Japan.
You can read this in Low's *Feral Future*.

He'll point you to Port Philip Bay,
to seaworms thick under the hulls
as windsock carp at a kite festival

afloat on dusk. Night falls as a blanket
on the comatose, a loose weave
of seastars yellow as congealing deep-fry.

3.

I'm not fox. Call me ningani.
I who was fox, I have crossed
through many nations,
through Eora and through Dharug.
I crossed into Wiradjuri.
I ate lamb warm from the womb.
I have tasted bettong, bilby
(sent offshore for their protection).
I have felt the willy willy
sand the tongue of Karenggapa.
Roadkill fed me
through Wangkangurru to Arrernte.
I've survived on litter bins.
I've dodged guns. Snubbed 1080.
Say ningani. Puwutjuma.
Show respect. I have my song.

4.

He curates fauna the most primitive on earth:
foolish marsupials, mere foetuses at birth,

grubs wriggling to their pseudo-wombs.
His copperplate puts a brave face

on ecological cringe: *animals of this class
must go down before invaders*

so far ahead in Darwinian terms
(Albert Le Souef, Taronga Park, 1923).

But inferiority's complex. Trees and shrubs
evolved on the eroded continent

promoted by aid agencies
lay claim to foreign lands farmed bare.

Wattle, silky oak, the casuarina's
fistfuls of nine inch nails

move in where vanished Africans
will never be repatriated.

Our wattles are exhausting
Cape Town's water with their thirst.

Expat melaleucas drink Miami swamps,
their shaggy manuscript rewriting highways.

5

The host dies; the gene endures. The product's obsolescence
is the trademark's strength, no time lost in the brief flutter
from C.A.D. to landfill wherein desires propagate
geometrically in endless Next Gens. Economies of scale
secure full penetration of the market garden habitat.
Local species go the way of corner stores;
niche retailers seek shiftwork in the same malls
where young acquire their must-have strains of affluenza.
Like mall rat casuals sugar gliding on cheap calories
our natives learn to live with, then rely on pests.
As far as the eye can't see, the heart won't grieve.
Delete your documentaries. Focus on the new nature.
Wear fast fashion. Look to thickets of lantana
for bandicoots and whipbirds, fairywrens and scrubwrens,
Richmond birdwing butterflies, insects colonising carcasses,
reed bees nesting in the stems. Believe that paperbark apologists
find raccoon road-kill, woodpeckers among their trees.
Take solace in the eucalypts that feed African cooking fires.
Do what you must. See what you will.
Ningani in the August heat takes cover in the blackberry.

Note:
This poem germinated in my reading of Tim Low's *Feral Future: The Untold Story of Australia's Exotic Invaders* (Penguin, 1999). The phrase 'the new nature' is Low's, as is the definition of Botanic Gardens as 'zoos for plants.' Any scientific errors in the poem are my own.

The Book of Crow
Steve Evans

1. On the First Day

On the first day,
Crow created Crow in its own image
and was satisfied.

There is no God of Crows.
but if there were,
Crow would not believe in it.

Even the youngest Crow
has an ageless stare
that reads your discomfort precisely.

The skull of Crow is small
but it is a library of every animal,
all weather, the stark plenty of the world.

Crow has constellations above,
the least insect below.
What need of gods?

2. Crow Facts

Crow always opens to the story of Crow.
Crow is dark pearl ink signing the sky.
Crow makes the rest of the world seem bright.
Crow can recall every mouse it has seen.
Crow humour is best kept for Crows.

Crow is a creature of its own devise.
Crow cannot be caught by false songs.
Crow taught lightning to dance.
Crow is blacker than the family Bible.
Crow has a High Street tailor make its suits.

Crow prays at the altar of new death.
Crow is the blade for the bone that calls to it.
Crow knows the eyes of lambs see it last.
Crow preaches sermons on the virtues of Crow.
Crow sits on top of the world.

3. *Crow on Fire*

Outwardly, Crow is
lacquered as if still wet,
a fine chinoiserie,
but Crow has heat beyond
its singularity.

At first no light escapes.
Crow is its own black hole
swallowing the smallest glimmer
of itself back into darkness,
into the space of Crow.

But it burns.
Crow is on fire within,
a delicate flame
the size of a bird's heart,
tenacious in its engine-room.

You might see it
when two or three together
glow in their bleak joy,
jointly glistening
the meaning of Crow.

4. *Crow's Sunday Service*

Though he thinks he's a sharp dresser,
    Crow is tatty today.
He clenches his fine claws
    tighter on the wire.
The drops of gone rain
    are jewels strung beside him.

Down on the wet ground
    is a small house
with an old woman inside
    whose speech has abandoned her.
He thinks he sings her voice now,
    though he keeps this to himself.

Crow will tidy his frock-coat
        and drop to her sill,
one of all things beautiful and bright,
        however dark, unkempt,
with his orison ready
        for a few stale crumbs of bread.

5. *Crow and Shadow*

Crow takes its shadow
to a place beside the road
and watches patiently
Crow says to shadow,
'Here is where our meal will fall.'
But night hauls in its blackness
and indifferent stars.
Crow sees that it is all alone.

In the morning sunlight,
shadow returns to Crow's side and asks,
'Where is our promised dinner?'
Crow only shakes its head.
Then, forgoing grace,
eats its shadow at a gulp.
There was nothing else to do.
Sometimes you take what you can get.

6. *Fox and Crow*

I am fire and grace in motion,
says Fox.
I have a pelt of unimagined beauty.
Crow does not speak.

I am the glamour and the glory,
says Fox.
I am a loner, free of my leash.
Crow does not speak.

I see the Earth's magnetic field,
says Fox.
It feeds and praises me.
Crow does not speak.

I made the Northern Lights,
says Fox.
My tail swept sparks into the sky.
Crow does not speak.

Fox settles on its paws
and waits,
twitches its famous ears.
Crow does not speak.

Crow tilts its head,
extends its wings' dark fans
and flies high above the dwindling Fox
without once looking down.

7. *No Crow*

Where ten of them might gather,
each one its own night,
comes only the lack of Crow.

Absences.
Outlines in the sky.
No darkness, where that darkness was.

What will Crow mean
in stories of brooding eclipse,
if we still speak them?

How will children tell their children
the time of Crow,
its before and after,

when Crow is gone,
in the no-Crow time?

They
Catherine Wright

For Wallamumbi

It would be cows. Sweet cows. And bulls with
presidential shoulders, terror's eyes
and thunder-throated calls for combat in the dusk
or the trumpeting of mum, cleaved from her calf
the old yards haunted by each cold abduction.
And will they remember wise, one-armed Bill
his good one up that kicker's arse; feel the skin?
She's empty, swing her to the left. Or John
Get-away-out-for-chrissakes-the-mob-is-running-
hot-the-Big-Fella-will-lose-it. About our dad.
Perhaps it would be the galloped powder cloud or
fly-flicked susurrus of tails at rest, or the poddy's
tongue frothed with milky need, square on to
guzzle each silky drop, the udder-bottle bunted
and elysium in his glossy eye.

But if I know them anymore, childrened now
now bent with choice, it will perhaps be that
clematis flower or stump worn smooth by hide
or clouds that purple above the range, summer
storms and diamond frosts, warm manure oozing
through pinkened toes, jasmine twining by the fern.
It will be cake, swelling hot with sugared crust
butter leaking from our reaching fingers.
It will be the phone, and dad's strong back turned
away to New Japan – for us or them or God
knows who – or turned towards, hair done in bows
laughing with those ocean eyes.

And it will be the beehive of our mother's hair
poised above her cloud-sway kaftan – a symphony
in nylon – she left behind four pale faces choked on
tears, Cedel hairspray and Dior, Holdened off
by dad in dust and tan, his precision part
knife-white beneath the moon, and some old trout
said Off to bed or else I'll tell your dad
then you'll be sad and sorry. And we were
we have been, sad and sorry for some time now.
It would be the way her body shrank to bones
and how his ox heart stopped one beat.
We left our home in sleet. They took
the keys, locked our doors and sold the cows.

In Perugia, November 1, 2007
Oliver Driscoll

That I cannot know what you want from me / That I cannot know what to make of my own appearance / That I cannot look myself up / That I cannot not / That even people who believe I am innocent tell me how to act / That even people who believe I'm innocent will say, but she doesn't seem very likeable / That they say, you should always mention *her* first / That I am warned pre-emptively against going on Dancing with the Stars / That no matter what I do, it means I'm guilty / That I needed the money / That to remain silent, would have been to hide something / That to say what I needed to say, was to draw attention to myself, away from the real victim / That there cannot be more than one victim / That there is a greater victim / That I was still in prison for four years / That I am tired of explaining confirmation bias / That the discussion will always continue / That for some, this is a crime to solve / That the forums are communities, of a kind / That if they had not found me guilty a second time / That if we had not kissed / That if I had known how to say 'see you later' so as to mean 'good bye' in Italian / That I cannot stop reading comments / That they can be so wilfully unseeing / That I cannot trust / That I cannot know if I'm doing what I'm doing because I would do it anyway or because I have a need to prove myself to people who have not proven themselves to me / That the killer will be out in three years / That sometimes I think I must be guilty of something / That people say, she's probably innocent, but she knows something / That people say, she said 'um' too many times / That people say, she nodded when she said 'no' / That people say, if I were innocent, I would talk faster, she is talking so slowly / That people say, it has nothing to do with her beauty, she's not even that beautiful / That I cannot be seen to be full of rage / That I cannot trust myself / That I have broken / That I incriminated an innocent black man / That I am forever tied to my nineteen-year-old self / That I have seen the worst of myself / That it should then feel clear, the climb upward / That it doesn't / That I suspect that I interview people who have had similar experiences because I'm not done with the conversation and yet cannot talk only about this / That I suspect this is a means of coping, of facing up to / That I don't know why people are drawn to me, and why they hate me / That I live with a version of myself who was never convicted, who hadn't kissed her boyfriend, who hadn't done the splits, who had known how to write 'see you later' so as to say 'good bye' in Italian / That I don't know what I would otherwise be doing / That no matter what I do, this will always have the greatest weight / That nothing can be written about me without this introduction / That the prosecutor must know what he's done / That the killer definitely knows what he's done / That his story is absurd / That some people think he's innocent / That, like the innocent man I incriminated, he is black / That some people sympathise with me because they feel as though they know me, or because they see themselves or their loved ones in me / That when you're told over and over that you're a stupid little liar you feel like a stupid little liar / That this is a platform I didn't ask for / That, as a nineteen-year-old, I was severely sexualised / That women have not always come to my defence, have not always recognised me as one of themselves / That life was briefly so rich / That I was blossoming / That I loved Italy / That I didn't know if I'd ever spend time with my family again / That I was so intelligent, and yet couldn't see what was happening around me / That I don't know if it's okay when someone wants something of me / That if I wear the wrong thing / That time goes so quickly / That time would have disappeared anyway, in or out of prison / That anyone can say what they like about me / That I love languages / That I want to travel / That I am good / That I care if people think of me as good / That I care / That I am scared / That I don't want to be alone / That there was blood in the downstairs apartment / That a pillowcase was soaked in it / That they said it was a cat / That the cat had a cut on its ear / That it didn't fit their story / That I have my defence ready for anyone who challenges me / That I don't want to have it ready / That I don't want it in my head / That once you've been picked over when you're too young to have substance, you will always feel as though you lack substance / That I can manifest controversy if I want to / That sometimes, like pressing a bruise, I want to / That sometimes I want rage swirling around me, to have something tangible to fight / That I feel I am not in possession of my own name / That when I returned to Italy people said, the killer always returns to the scene of the crime / That I could have been one of those people / That I wanted cultural immersion / That I got it / That I should feel lucky / That I know how easy it is to reframe a story / That I can feel myself doing it / That I never thought I would be convicted / That I wasn't ready / That no one ever is / That sometimes it feels that the types of people who believe me to be guilty would like me more if I were a killer / That I think there are types / That I don't always like myself either / That this is always new to somebody / That my defence is a lot less succinct and compulsive than saying, what about the confession, what about the luminol footprints / That once you are a character, once people are paying you a particular kind of attention, everything you do can only be performance / That I liked her / That she was the kind of person you wanted to be / That we didn't know each other well but were friends or were becoming friends / That when I say I was a child, I was a child / That I wanted my mum / That when I find myself sobbing I don't know who or what I'm crying for / That being a young white woman who was seen to be attractive worked both for and against me / That the disconnect between what I seemed to be and what I was accused of doing was what was so compelling and alarming / That being a cluster of concepts or perfect examples is yet another form of erasure / That I don't know what I did with the four years I spent in prison / That if I knew I was going to get out / That, as a culture, we revel in violence, particularly it seems to me, violence towards women / That we feast on it / That since November 1st, 2007, over 10,000 women have been killed by their partners in my country / That you wouldn't know it / That they say, she's just like Ted Bundy / That Ted Bundy wouldn't have, as I did, drawn attention to himself / That no one would have accused Ted Bundy of lying / That *her* family wants me imprisoned for life / That in some way the TV drama of it gets into everything and everyone, including my family, my friends / That I made a friend in poetry class / That when I dress playfully I don't know if I'm doing so because I want to or because that's what I think I would have done if this had never happened / That I will never be that self / That I'm glad I won't / That I suffer / That others suffer / That there are people I was in prison with who are still there / That I am white / That my beauty was forced on to me / That I can't take pleasure in it / That if I had not kissed / That if I had not said 'ta da' / That if I hadn't believed them when they'd said a lawyer would only make things worse / That sometimes I want to be admired / That I've worked hard / That some people say, just wait until she does it again / That they say, if I were innocent, I'd hide away in my house / That even my husband might like that I'm an exoneree / That people obsess over some deaths, while ignoring the rest / That if they believe you to be guilty, they would be doing right in their minds to focus on evidence that seems to incriminate you, while ignoring the rest / That I am happy / That I've found love / That I know how quickly it can be taken / That I don't know what my friends have read about me / That my father cried / That I have family / That if I hadn't been let out, I would have been willing to kill for my release / That not everyone turned against me / That I thought it was over once I was released / That it will never be over, not entirely / That there are cats /

draft [1] [two]
Christine Fontana

which was the same year she went to Spain to write the novel that would define her career and herald a new and successful era

during which year she did not hear from her son for three months and having not heard decided to book her [sad] ticket to Spain where she would write the novel that would

after not hearing from her son for four months decided to pack up the small room she rented in a St Kilda rooming house and travel to Spain to write the

that was the year she took refuge from uncertainty in the rooming house owned by such [generous] friends as allowed her to be there, where being it is said her first genre novel was written in an attempt to make commercial hay while the sun still shone, and is famously quoted as having said not even Rumplestiltskin could make hay from this [shit], funny because the sun didn't [much], shine

the year she had almost booked her ticket and [almost] gone back to Spain to finish her most promising novel but was told by the boss at her shit-kicking job that she was not allowed to take annual leave at this present time

having died so tragically young that year in which she travelled to Spain to earn the right to die early by finishing the novel that was designed to be her fond farewell to life

after living to a ripe old age having earned the right to live that year during which she travelled to Spain to finish the novel that was to be a fond [but only symbolic] farewell to her old life thus enabling her to move on with the new [life] after the unexpected experience of things [for once] going inexplicably [for once] right

the year during which her career was launched by the posthumous success of the novel she wrote in Spain due to the brilliant marketing value of her [untimely] death having earned the right to not-die by travelling to Spain to appease the life gods with her energy and exuberant will to live through writing the novel that was the last barrier between her and her future

after travelling to Spain that year to finish the novel about the man [but not really] who filled her so much with life [he] [it] made her want to die – which she later did – which she did not yet

the decision to not quit her job to return to Spain to write her novel [not] about the Spanish man, demonstrating latent maturity and [finally] fiscal responsibility, allowing her to fulfil her dream of living a conventional and [therefore] secure life

the year during which she would quit her job so that she could go to Spain to write her [anyway] novel [anyway], having not yet learned the Spanish word for conven[c]ional and lacking in [the same] fiscal maturity that led to her having to take refuge in the generous rooming house of [such] generous friends who

her lack of belief in her own ability no more evident than in her choice to stay with her kitchen job where once she would have quit and gone to Spain anyway [saying] screw you I have a book to write, which she did not say but only would have [once], hence the evident maturity herein demonstrated

having that year summoned the courage to not go to Spain – yet – was to learn sadly that not going to Spain to write the most promising novel of her career left potential publishers without a valuable marketing byte for the future promotion of the novel she was or was not able to successfully write

the year she travelled back to Spain to write one novel but accidentally wrote another which projected her into instant publishing [though not of the literary sort] success which saw her finally able to buy a small apartment wherein to make [more] hay [funny]

is survived by a son who did not know she was going to go to Spain and therefore did not know that she didn't go to Spain after all, was merely here as opposed to not being there and therefore it could not be remembered and was a year that pales in comparison to the years before during which she loved a Spanish man so much she wanted to write a novel about him that wasn't really about him [at all] and is famously quoted as saying even Rumplestiltskin couldn't make love out of this [shit]

is survived by a sometimes daughter who refused to look after Cat when she went to Spain to work on the novel that would define her career and make her inadvertently a better mother through the virtue of success, meaning she [would not have] wasted her life so far

never did write that novel [not] about the Spanish man, or eventually did during which year she travelled every day [instead] to the library to write [a novel] but it was so bad [having suffered from not being written in Spain] she was relieved not to have quit her job for the sake of [it] despite the [unkind] boss who [fuck you] wouldn't let her take annual leave even though she had [fuck] three years owing due to her lack of earlier readiness for Spain as such

is survived by a sometimes daughter who cannot be mentioned except during such times as her daughterness is not in dispute, hence the need for Spain and the writing of novels in places removed from life wherein locality is a brutal reminder of the [sometimes] suffering inherent within

during [finally] which year [this] she [untimely] died due to unspecified circumstances related to [shit-kicking] responsibilities that prevented her from going to Spain to find a reason to live

during which time she stayed at her place of employment where she will be sadly missed as a valued member of the team, where she will be sadly remembered, has been forgotten already such is the nature of that [not Spanish] place and its having not allowed her to go to Spain to write the novel that would keep her [forever] in our minds and [therefore] hearts

The Silk Moth Cannot Fly
Joanne Ruppin

his mother's words float past him
too soft to land
    The silk moth cannot fly
she slides her fingers over his
drives them through lanes of thin ribbons
along his new brother's gown
    A baby silkworm has no life without us

his hand slips from hers
cools when it ripples over silk frets
the baby is a strange little brother
draped in white
his own pink fingers tippy-toe across a pleated glacier
nudge through his mother's words
and land
at a balled dry hand
his brother's hand
it's not a proper brother
not the brother he'd been waiting for
not a brother to play with
this brother never moves

this brother has stolen his mother's lap

his mother's voice takes off
and spins lacy loops of lullaby over and over and over
and crashes
she scratches at a strand of tune
smudges the edge
messes it
the lullaby unravels
she spreads her hands over her face
and crumples inside the big chair
there are valleys in the silk gown
where her hands were
there is crying
where the lullaby was

his mother's tears drip
through the valleys

he moves his hand from the damp
finds a cool silk space
to hold pain

he asks why
why his brother does nothing
why his brother lulls in her lap
wrapped in white
Where did it come from
all this white?
she's broken her voice
he stares at her lips to hear her
      This is the gown you once wore
Before I was a boy
when I was a baby?
      When you were just born
he folds silk inside his palm
Why was my gown taken from me?
Why was it given to my brother?
he squeezes the silk
white oozes between knuckles
      You were strong You grew and grew
      too big for the gown
Have I stopped growing?
      You won't stop growing
she looks at his little brother
fusses at a frill
scrapes her throat for a thread of lullaby

he pats his brother's curled fist
cold hits him
hurts him
he feels for a warm space on the gown
away from his brother's fist
calls through his mother's song

Where does it come from
the shiny whiteness?
Where will it go?
she shuts her eyes and talks in bumps
about smooth pale caterpillars
and mulberry leaves
and magic babies who live whole lives
in weeks
he grabs her hand from where she's left it
dangling outside her chair
their hands glide over slippery skirt
share stripes of shadow and light
>*So small so small when they are born*
>*they can't forage, we must feed them*

Feed?
>*Just a little at first*
>*they eat and grow out of their skin*

Are all skins the same?
>*The boy smaller than the girl*

his mother lifts her other hand and cups his
together they ride the gown's long sash
>*Gently, softness can bruise*

she slows their hands
>*When the skin doesn't fit anymore*
>*they take it off*
>*a new skin is waiting*

her words dip
>*Some never grow*

she's looking for tears again
he hurries and fills the space

Do they give the old skin to their brother?
she picks at a frayed song
pinches fluff from his brother's collar
drags her fingers over lumps of pintucking
>*No one else's skin can fit*

Mine might
>*It never does*

her lips are on his brother's cheek
it's not a kiss
it's where she stirs words and lullaby and tears
into watery sound
    We must use the skin we have
Does he like his new skin, the caterpillar?
the watery sound covers her
he pushes dimples into the silk near her voice
pulls her back
    New skin is what's needed
her fingers flit around the edge of a shawl
a silk wave settles over his brother
whiter than the high clouds of summer
she lifts the baby and wraps the silk wave
round and round and round him
    The caterpillar spins a creamy silk cocoon
    around itself

all that is left of the brother is a face
mottled by twilight
mottled in twilight
    Precious cocoon
Precious?
    More so than gold
he strokes the swaddled cocoon
When will the caterpillar wake?
his mother brushes his arm
away from the cocoon
she cradles the brother against her chest
    He loses his skin in the cocoon
Again?
    For the last time
But when he grows?
    There is no eating in the cocoon
    no growing
When will he play?
    This one will never play
she finds her melody
    The silk moth cannot fly

The Lost Man
Frank Leggett

So, this ¿policeman? is grabbing me by the neck
Yelling in Spanish
Angry as Hell
Español de secundaria
Means I get the essence of his acrimony
Then he punches me in the throat

Fucker

Why am I even thinking about this?
I should be concentrating on (name withheld), my wife
She is in full cry, cataloguing

                  All (155.232)

                  My (362.292)

                  Shortcomings (306.736)

And then she is gone with a slam of the door and nary a backwards glance

I feel a moment of relief
                  of lightness
But that is momentary

                Für (name withheld)

                here is where I fell
          this is where the blood drained
                the pump froze
            the disassembling began
      this is the exact spot where I became
              el hombre perdido

                come, take my hand
      let me show you around the exhibition
        though mortified by the imbroglio
                I'll censor nothing
                nor lie by omission
                honestly, mi amigo

here are the pebbles,
each slightly larger than the preceding
they filled my empty spaces
weighing me down
slowing my speed
that calculous mound of lies

nearby, the blades
careful! they are honed to a fine degree
yet could cudgel the most reasonable exchange
until it was unrecognisable
just scattered blood and gore
on an impervious pavement

don't forget the hooks!
essential to keep the participants
engaged in the battle dance
… the fine romance
… the hypnotic trance
from which disengagement was unthinkable

but enough of the peripherals
let's get to the heart of the matter
poke it with a stick, use the pointy end!
have no fear, it can't bite anymore
the carcass is mort, devoid of thought
and bad intentions

if it gets too much
feel free to exeunt stage right
and leave this mound of flesh
this wreck of the Hesperus
this smoking ruin of a cruel bastard
The shell that is the lost man

It's so bad. So so bad. I should rip it up but…

I made that. I'll file it for future reference
Get it into shape and enter a few of those poetry competitions
Bit of money to be won there

I feel a need to create… to bring something into this world

Koestler
that old cock-knocker
said that creativity is the defeat of habit by originality

                                                I couldn't agree more, sir!

That fucking Ikea bookcase has been laying there for ages
Defying me to complete it
Bibs and bobs strewn across the floor
Assaulting my feet on a daily basis

I remember when (name withheld) and I purchased it
We zig-zagged through Ikea
With all the other zombies

                oohing and ahhing
                                    at the exhibition rooms

I'd had a vasectomy that very morning
The nurse was all black hair and smoky eyes
And I've always liked 'em a bit gothy
When she shaved me, I had a Costanza moment - It moved!
I was terrified of the story she would share
With laughing nurses and doctors
About the guy who cracked a stiffy before his vasectomy
Madre de Dios, I was at half-mongrel!
What to do? What to do?

Then Gothy stuck a syringe into my scrotum and the problem just
                                                  ...disappeared

But now I'm in Ikea
The anaesthetic is wearing off
And we're arguing about bookcases

I want Klimpen. Simple. Small. White.
She wants Havsta. In black. With a plinth.

The racking stretches to the roof, or maybe the moon
She spies Havsta boxes three levels up
I climb the racking
While Ikea goons yell at me
Making all kinds of threats

					But I fucking get it down, eh

My balls feel like they've swollen to the size of mangoes
Kensington Pride!
But the Ikea goons have no sympathy
They plonk me on a trolley and push me to the car

With Havsta
					In black
											With a plinth

Yeah, yeah, I started but never finished
It's been, what, a few weeks
Maybe 4, or 5
Maybe a bit more
I attack Havsta with renewed energy
I will create a bookcase where no bookcase has stood before!
I persevere until I nearly fucking impale my hand on a screwdriver
This motherfucking piece of shit Havsta is going out on the street!

											I'll get myself a Klimpen
I'll do it tomorrow
											Have a good feed of
Swedish meatballs
					15 for $10.95
											You can't beat that!

Then she's back
She's met up with my old girlfriend at the pub
They've been drinking chardonnay and swapping war stories
They're laughing and tipsy and having a great time
I offer coffee but they want Baileys
And then they start on me

Did he make you watch Star Trek?
											YES!
Me too
											It's so bad!
I could shit a better TV series!

Where does all this hate for Star Trek come from? Its accolades are many.

1. First interracial kiss.
2. Woman in command roles.
3. Foreigners as equals.
4. Peace.
5. Positive…

Oh, fuck off. You only watched for those sexy green aliens wearing fuck all and dancing like hornbags in harem pants.

> He's as transparent as a sheet of glass!

I don't need this
I retire to the back balcony
A little Maker's Mark takes off the edge
I break out the old photo album

> One photo
> Shows an impossibly young me
> In the Plaça de Catalunya
> In Barcelona
>
> I had spent the day at Nova Icaria Beach
> Swimming and floating in the sea
> While some mongrel stole the money
> Hidden in my shoe
> Leaving me destitute
>
> So, I got a job in a hostel
> Rounding up gormless backpackers
> And bringing them back to The Hipstel
>
> I got paid a pittance
> I was working illegally
> But I had no choice

And that was when the throat punching ¿policeman?
Threatened arrest
And put the fear of god into me

I sat in Ciutadella Park
I had no money
I had no credit cards
I couldn't work anymore
What was I gonna do?

Well, sometimes the universe is kind
Sometimes fate smiles on you
Sometimes stupid fuckers are very lucky

I saw them first
Two female backpackers
Walking through the park
Laughing and chatting
Not a care in the world

They looked in my direction
I raised a hand in greeting
They came over
Are you okay? You look a little…
What?

                                                            …terrified

One was American. One was Australian. They bought me lunch.
And a cold cerveza. And gave me some money. And we traveled together.
And, eventually, I was able to pay them back.

LONG STORY, SHORT
Over a period of ten years, I dated one but married the other

Now, they were sitting in my kitchen
Laughing and talking and drinking
When I re-entered, they smiled and said

                                             We're out of Baileys

Allow me to replenish! I said
Grabbing my wallet
The bottle shop
My destination

                                    I mean, Jesus, why wouldn't I?

I'm glad you asked me that
Owen Bullock

you see, a crocodile has three rows of teeth in
    case it loses any of the front ones (and to strengthen
        the jaw, especially the lower mandibles)
most balloons go sideways first and then up but do it
    so quickly you don't notice
when fish that can hibernate in dried ponds realise
    they can't move any longer, about to
        go into a suspended state, they make
            gentle but prolonged sounds some biologists call
        the sleep song
when you take your glasses off your eyes adjust
    within five seconds, exactly twice as quick as when
        you put them on
if you feel the gums of a gift horse it'll likely have
    a bit of a nip of your finger
if you take disinfectant for coronavirus, suing the company
    that made it for not supplying a label
        warning of the danger should cover
            your medical expenses
if you cross a horse with a dog you get a pig
if you read The Odyssey backwards it spells *I'm*
    in love with middle-aged white guys
if you go to the fountain in the middle of Kensington
    Gardens and press the base of the pedestal
        between the crack and the chip
            an assistant will bring you a cup of tea
                and a trained kestrel a small friand
if you're painting and you put green over blue
    it turns orange
if you play Led Zeppelin IV three times before dawn
    at Stonehenge a lake will open up and you
        can dive in, swim to the bottom and retrieve
            Aleister Crowley's fishing rod
if you write a story about a turtle with the power of
    speech you'll see one next day (no
        guarantees it'll say much to you
            on first meeting)

   if you hang a greatcoat up in the wardrobe for 60 days
          in exactly the same place a memory of
                   your brother will appear as a hologram
                         hovering at the shoulder
   if you tell him you love him from the urn of ashes that's never been
                                                     scattered
        he'll answer back

And Cyrus Wept When He Beheld Babylon
Peter Ramm

I

Cyrus, enraged at the insolence of the river,
threatened so to break its strength
—Herodotus, Histories

> *May what I do flow from me like a river,*
> *no forcing and no holding back,*
> *the way it is with children.*
> **— Rainer Maria Rilke**

A torrent, the Wingecarribee in flood,
          As if Van Gogh had painted the night sky across its surface.
On the horizon, three pied cormorants climb a cumulus shroud out of the wetlands,
     Their wings like dishevelled dress coats. In the reserve, a river box stands
Low and pregnant with rain and sweeps the wind from the river.
    A snow gum—
          Its bark a matted mane—is submerged like Cyrus's Nisaean
              Stallion in the stream, and stuck:
                      Pale, sacred, drowning.

The woodlands watch—a thousand spearmen in despair.
    Ambition, the eighth sin, weighs in the storm what it weighs
        In the silence of a landscape in its new skin—
            This place, like all places, is naked after rain.
        And mist peels from the water.

When Cyrus raged, he took the river and left her
    In three hundred and sixty pieces of herself
—And so it is between us sometimes. This afternoon, the weir
    Is a cacophonous cascade at the lagoon's edge, Beethoven's
Moonlight Sonata, stirring like the argument that parts us.
      Sometimes peace
          Is a phrase that's hard to place, a dependent clause
              Lost in the surge, the flotsam in a deluge
                  That jags on the reeds.

In the distance, a pair of straw-necked ibis stalk the sodden ground,
    Their feathers a map of unconquered worlds in the falling light.
        I know my mind is a workplace I never leave—impenetrable
           As the Ishtar Gate.

II
I am Cyrus: King of the Earth; Great King; Rightful King;
King of Babylon; King of the Four Quarters of the Earth
                                        Today, I must unlearn everything
                                          —like the swamphen in the storm,
                                      like the father who holds a newborn.

In his *paridaida* at Pasargadae, Cyrus taught his son to roam
                        The four quadrants of the world, through cypress and pomegranate
—The mad king skipping stones in the canals. On the porticos
           The light of the crescent moon ascending above swathes of grassland
And the milky way strung across the sky like the iris of God's great eye.
           A blood-built paradise
                      —The cherry orchard in a soft hue,
                                Their buds like a quiver of arrows.
                                                    The smell of jasmine

In the evening and Cambyses walking the banks of the Pulver
              With his mother, the crown victim in waiting. Cyrus, is holding court
                      In the columned hall, Babylon on his mind, and a kestrel
                      Hovers the open field.

It's late now. On a blackwood a cicada skin is shed like a past
                       Self—like a memory I'm trying peel from the inside. Slow,
Like the work of a poem, like the work of unravelling syllables.
            He'd left emptiness where a heart should be, his black wings singing no more
Over Bong Bong. In the carpark a plaque reads, "original settlement"
                  And the mud map bears four rough lines;
                          The only epitaphs for a hundred lives.
                          To mark the military post,
                                             A stone obelisk

Is flanked by the stumps of Lombardy poplars planted by Prince
              Richard in 1947—everything in decay, a radiata pine has collapsed
                    On the barbed fence line. The road from Babylon
                    Was always long.

III
Cyrus drained the Euphrates, so that it was passable on foot
and the Persians went in under Babylon's walls.
                                      My father's office was full of books
                                      like a dam wall—his love, the reservoir,
                                      a spillway in drought or flashing in the fall.

That hot night, Belshazzar, gorging on golden cups
                Found soldiers pitched in the shadows of Nebuchadnezzar.
The city asleep, dying by the river; a south wind
        Blowing in the date palms and Cyrus, the winged lion, ascending
The Etemenanki. It was Yahweh that warned; Mene, Mene, Tekel,
              —You have been weighed and found wanting.
                        This, the way of those who seek kingdoms
                                For themselves and raise monuments
                                          Instead of children.

Far, in Parsa, Cyrus's home had many faces:
            Mountain fog in the Zagros, Orion above she-oak silhouettes,
                And the bulrushes in obeisance to the flow.
                        There are other faces a father knows, I find:

Like the boy adrift on his pillow, the toothless cries of a newborn,
                Or the swarming joy of a toddler at afternoon's door.
Downstream the paddocks hug the riverbank and tussock grasses
           Besiege the floodplain—their fingers combing the air for its fortune.
At the edges, silver banksias brandish their fat cigars
           And clouds rise in the branches
                      —Old men in a smoke room.
                          The banjo frog plucks the last strings of daylight
                                  And the coming dark scatters

The image of my son, who's blowing dandelions
              At his brother's face. Moths linger like moments of yesterday,
                  Drawn to me like grief's return—the land in a state of perpetual undress,
                      The rain strips what she wishes.

IV
Were it not disgrace intolerable for Cyrus
to retire before and yield ground to a woman?
                                My love, spun like a spider's silk line
                                    —a logarithmic curve in the wind, bent
                     under the weight of the sky; teardrops on a clothesline.

Late summer, the plums creep into blackness, tamarix petals fall
             Like droplets on the terrace and the shape of mourning sets in the boughs
Of the pear trees, heavier in fruit and shadow. Cyrus in the gardens,
          His daughters bear the news of Cassandane—an empire drawn in sackcloth.
Two hoopoes call from the rock wall, a trisyllabic oop-oop-oop; that loss
                  That makes refugees of us all,
                        Like foreigners in our own bodies.
                              The funeral chariot passes
                                      Through the streets of Babylon,

The children, orphans of desire. Cedar, nightshade, willow;
            The roots and soil know their own, but we are condemned travellers
                —The wind blows the same as it always has, over
                    A thousand faces in the sand.

The windscreen wipers see rain in the offing, Moss Vale in May,
                  The moon rising on one side is wet and cold, the grass an unfurled
Patchwork quilt. In the tufts a fox pads its paws in silence,
          Its tail combing a heavy fog, fluffed and floating into a hollow.
Life in its long migration, learning to yield to the season;
                In autumn, in the first breaths of winter
                      On the mat rush—stems glistening
                            Like medieval maces. Two yellow-faced honeyeaters
                                  Tuck into an iron bark for the night,

The highway hums onwards and the steering wheel pulls me home.
           In the driveway each steppingstone is repentance,
                 A prayer—grace in the lowness of our hearts; slender consolation.
                 White egrets asleep in the marsh.

V

On the death of her son, Queen Tomyris sent a messenger to Cyrus,
'I will give thee thy fill of blood, insatiable as thou art.'
                                          The children asleep, we sip from the same cup
                                            And taste each other again—skin and bone,
                                      We leave our imprints in the minutes of night.

You prepared a table before your enemies, laid it with wine,
        Pomegranates, grape, and a slaughtered lamb; how quick birth rights are lost
For warm flesh. Tomyris's prince, young leopard with ambition—the black iris
        Of man's eyes, those dark supernovae of the soul. Stratus clouds
Over a ribbon lake, like a pale coffin pall
                —Alpine swifts on the wing in the fingers of mountain light.
                    Cyrus continues his relentless warring
                          And leaves his own in Babylon—there's always work
                                In the mind's empire,

Always the job of today. Tomyris's army on the river,
        Preti will find his inspiration—the warrior queen,
                Stoops to drown Cyrus's head in the blood bag,
                        His all-consuming work—Babylon will weep again.

Tomorrow, I'll follow the child in the garden and look to correct his tantrum;
                Legs flailing like a two-foot drunk conductor—he'll be throwing rocks
Across the lawn. But a smile will betray me, and he'll know
        The kookaburra in the Northfoke Pine is recruited to his cause.
On the border, the peace rose will stubbornly out-flower the black spot
        And shower the rock wall
With petals and perfume. Lime-sulphur
                Will leave a milk white skin on the myrtle,
                              —Mildew will leave the same.

All things in their temporal sphere—rosellas with their blood dipped breasts
        Sail under the powerlines and I will sit with my son in the lap
                Of the afternoon, drawing treasure maps in the dirt,
                        Doing love's work among the maple leaves.

Notes:
- 'the night sky' alludes to Van Gogh's *Starry Night*.
- The Snow Gum, *Eucalyptus pauciflora*, isn't typically found in the Wingecarribee, but the low-lying topography of Cecil Hopkins Reserve creates a micro-climate in which it can survive.
- The Nisean Stallion refers to an extinct breed of horse that was renown in the ancient world. Bred in Media, pure white Nisean horses were chosen by the Persian king Xerxes to pull the chariot reserved for the god Ahura Mazda and for his own. Herodotus records that eight Nisean horses were used for the Ahura Mazda's chariot and the charioteer walked behind the empty as no mortal was permitted to sit in the carriage. The horses were famed for their size and speed.
- 'unlearn everything' from Charles Wright's *Watching the Equinox Arrive in Charlottesville, September 1992*. 'Where each year the orchid unlearns everything it's been taught.'
- *Paridaida*, Old Persian, 'walled around' ie. a walled garden. The root word for the Latin paradisus and English paradise. The gardens were characterised by a central canal system that divide the space into four quadrants by four 'rivers.' It was intended to represent the Abrahamic notion of the Garden of Eden and the four corners of the world. This style became a feature that was a central element in the design of Persian gardens, whose legacy on garden design extends to this day in many cultures and famous sites, including the Taj-Mahal in India. Cyrus and Cambyses are known in history as the conquering fathers of the Persian empire, having subdued the four great empires that proceeded the rise of the Persians: the Median, Lydian, Babylonian and Egyptian empires.
- *Hoopoes* have long and rich cultural tradition in many civilisations. Here chosen for their references in Sufi poet Farid ud-Din Attar's Persian poem *The Conference of the Birds* as the wisest of the birds. In Persia they were seen as a symbol of virtue and in Minioan Crete as emblematic of the crown prince. In the Quran the hoopoe is a diviner of knowledge to Solomon.
- *He's left emptiness where a heart should be, his black wings sing no more* | riffs on Charles Wright's *Cicada* "No song but the song of his black wings, | such emptiness at heart."
- Belshazzar the regent king of Babylon who fell to Cyrus in 539BC. Mentioned in the Biblical *Daniel* as the king who receives the 'writing on the wall.' The golden cups were said to be from the first Jewish Temple of Yaweh.
- The Banjo frog, named for the poet and of Mark Tredinnick's *Margaret River Sestets* 'strings loose as a gossip's tongue.'
- 'Moss Vale in May. The moon rising on one side is cold and wet' this stanza plays on Heaney's *Postscript*, "Into County Clare, along the Flaggy Shore | In September" and "Their feathers roughed and ruffling, white on white"
- Queen Tomyris' son, Spargapises, was captured in a ruse by Cyrus and his commanders, who had feigned a retreat and laid a feast for the pursuing army. On the tables were lavished with wine and food, the former something the Scythian tribes were not accustom to drinking. Once drunk, the Persians ambushed Spargapises and his men, capturing him alive and killing many of the others. Spargapises convinced Cyrus to release him, but committed suicide, thus bringing on the vengeful wrath of Queen Tomyris and by extension, the symbolic drowning of Cyrus head in a blood-filled wine sack.
- Mattia Preti, an Italian Baroque artist of the 17th Century painted a series on Queen Tomryis who, by legend is the one who defeated Cyrus in battle and fulfilled her own prophecy by placing his head in a wine sack filled with blood.
- Love's work, plays on Mark Tredinnick 'grief's work.'

Vase
Joe Dolce

Charred French hunting horn,
hooking a stump,
roofing tin twisted by Brâncuși,
glass heat-fused to plates,
crockery powdered to mosaic,
handleless garden tools.
Every inside now an outside.

Standing in the ruins of the home,
raking through rubble,
looking for a whole anything,
the house which held many objects of memory,
now itself a memory,
memories consumed by memory.

A hand-made stone chimney stands,
towering unsteadily, punch-drunk,
still on its feet, although no one can see how,
its gape-mouthed gargoyle hearth,
splintered and battered.
Why do chimneys survive bush fires?
Is it quiet understanding between
the small ritual fire place –
our human offering -
and the great devouring Fire God,
some recognition of kin?

Remnants of a river stone painted by a granddaughter
we haven't seen in six years.
Half a pottery head thrown by a son
who no longer speaks to us,

and a handful-sized round vase,
its O-mouth of wonderment,
sitting undamaged in the epicentre.

Ephemera
Audrey Molloy

I would carry the shell with me for years,
pressing the spindle to my fingertip
   with the precision of a type-1 diabetic
     or the sharp truth of Neruda:
'Love is so short. Forgetting so long.'
I'd since repaired the sleeve of the crane-
   print kimono that arrived with his letter,
     the one I wore on the day of Great Undoing.
I'd brought him a gift,
a pair of Hyacinth macaws
   that knew a bird when they saw one
     and settled at once on his shoulders.
He'd brought me a rare tibia fusus
from the floor of the Red Sea,
   a spirelet housed in a beaded purse.
     I knew his soul quite intimately,
but not how he took his tea (white),
or how he laughed like a pirate,
   stirring the birds to mild consternation.
     We drank pastis under the lattice of a shack,
the Seven Sisters just visible over trees
where goats played hide-and-seek.
   We were perspiring from the journey,
     or it could have been from nerves.
We didn't make love, or even kiss,
and, though it was the solstice,
   the night was endless, a Möbius strip
     that looks, when later cast aside,
a little like the aperture of a rare shell
or a ruptured human heart.

        *

I had wanted a solid existence, like an éclair
piped with crème pâtissière,
   the kind I learned to make
     from a hotel chef in Limoges,
where I worked, one year, as kitchen hand.
His room was veiled in maidenhair

    that cast a net of sunlight where we lay
      translating Nina Simone.
I preferred Paul Simon, and so
I sent him a monogrammed Zippo
    inlaid in scrimshaw. I imagine he kept it,
      in a shoebox with cassette tapes
and a few onionskin letters in bad French.
I recalled his umami-scented hands for years,
    whenever I prepared an omelette
      from day-old eggs stored overnight
in an airtight box with a knob of truffle.
They lie next to each other—
    seahorse hippocampus, almond amygdala
      and olfactory bulb, laid out like ingredients
        for gremolata, or regret.

        *

There's a word in Scots Gaelic called *sgrìob*,
which refers to the tingle
   on your upper lip
     just before you take a sip of whiskey.
We are talking, after the burial,
now they've allowed funerals again,
    across a table no bigger than a dinner plate
      about who we've lost to the virus,
and *whiskey* or *whisky*, the important things,
when 'Sweet Dreams' comes on the jukebox
    and I can almost taste the light
      film of sweat on his skin.
I should have known it right then:
an inventor will always be curious,
    and that here, in this bar, months from now,
      he will sit in false darkness
with another muse,
while on our white-board veranda,
    its double swing written by Harper Lee,
      I'll dip my best bristle brush
in tin after tin of green—
    viridian, sap, olive, Prussian—
      and slap paint mixed with salt onto timber shades
        until every trace of off-white is erased.
I'll forgive him, in time, everything

but the way he changed my name,
   in the song that made him famous,
      trimming a syllable to rhyme with *began*;
the irony of that, since it was the end,
and not even our story,
   though all unhappy stories resemble each other.
   But stop! We're getting ahead of ourselves,
haven't yet begun, and right here and now,
in The Fiddler's Arms,
   there's a feeling coming over me,
      a surface tension close to my upper lip,
         that no English word can describe.

Sticks 'N' Stones
Tug Dumbly

1. Stick

I cop a nervous eye swinging
a stick down Glebe Point Road.
No menace meant, ma'am.

I can't pass a nice limb
without fondling its physics.

Some sprite in the wood
invites me to pendulum thinking,
to pivot the wrist and dowse the blood
like a diviner
          walk, swing, cane the thing
sweet whackulator
animating some balancing act
in my nature.

Tongue with a thumb
that stubbled rough,
braille a bud, finger a groove,
get tactile as Barry White
with that stick & stickability

scab bark from its knee,
prawn shell it back
to clean white flesh,
to silken caress of a joint
duck-arse Tally-Hoed

or string it like a green bean,
strip veins from the limb
down to callow bone.

No don't be alarmed now ma'am,
it's just the thrill of the whittler
whipping a willow,
swooshing a gum club,

striping impertinent air
with a bamboo rattan.

I'm just mucking here,
golfing a coke can,
stabbing a chip wrapper
with the sticky beak
of my oyster catcher,
xylophoning a fence
in a small unlicensed show
of urban exuberance.

Unless it's Bush we go
then Whoosh! sword bracken,
brokeback weed, breaking bad a path
through that bleeding green fecundity
like Sinatra swinging hard
through the jungle with a
sharp tongued Lantana Turner.

And then when done
fling that stick
like it longs to be flung,
with the centrifugal begging of a dog,
end over end, ape-thrown bone, ass-jaw boomerang.

Kiss my primal arse
with your sheeny cane
and Joycey ashplant, with your
prissied, bevelled mansmoothed bat.
Get me to grips with a good stick, with
where it all began.

2. Stone

I can't leave a rock unfisted,
a stone untexted, but must
Gutenberg press it to skin,
cuneiform its imprint to palm

of clay, weigh the cooled
magma tongue of a pebble
in wallet of flesh, wombed
like a coin in a vending slot

snailed to forefinger,
sprung to sinew
of the wrist's slingshot,
a trebuchet drawn back

like Russell Crowe full cocked:
'at my signal, unleash hell ...'
Go on son, have a fling,
show us whatcha got –

Ah, the kinetic cleanse
of a raw chucked rock!
jemmying a rainbow,
pinchin' gravity like a fat

child's cheek, to crack a gum,
bounce from a pond,
be gulped like a frog
in the gob of a creek.

There's not always grace
but can be spectacle
to the Neolithic Games,
as a pair of bushboys lob

sandstone clods from a cliff
into a Tom Roberts afternoon, and
Bailed Up
       they sail
              the ravine
with the aim
of a Dresden bombardier
payload floating to the bedrock below

and oh the rapture as those
golden chunks of honeycomb
explode, in a violent crumble
of a most sweetly satisfying nature.

The Letter Carrier
Jo Gardiner

He walks across the spinning world,
his mind and feet such close companions.
He walks into dry country
until it seems the days themselves walk.

Possessed of an unshakeable devotion
to the act of walking,
he walks to his centre
and back again.
In light and in wind and in rain
he makes a long song of walking
across great open fields of solitude.

As he nears Ararat,
watching the road unroll before him
the sky turns the same lavender as the hills,
wildflowers appear in white and blue clusters,
purple patches across sandstone gorges and riverines.
He keeps an eye out for the tiny native orchids
in the shade of acacias, and for pink
and orange peas out in the sun.

Near the Grampians,
kangaroos mob at a creek
and four horses lift their heads in unison
to watch his progress.
Another canters off,
rippling like a cloud shadow over a barley crop,
tail and mane nothing more than light flickering
in and out of smoke and haze
and dry grass, hair the same texture
and colour of that grass.
The creature's passage across the paddock
moves something within him,
turns something over, licks at his insides.
The country's dry and waits for rain.
A dead stump stands like a torso in the paddock.
Others are more like frocked priests.

Trees lie where they've been felled,
limbs flung out above the head,
resting on a tussocky sea of yellow grass.

From their fence, eight crows
seem to be waiting for him
to drop down dead.

A hot wind springs up
and throws hordes of dusky swifts about,
blows dust into his eyes.
A grey horse close to the fence
snorts in the wind.
A windmill winds its blades,
grateful for motion.
Fences lean into the breeze
and he shudders,
remembering the monotony
of life on the land
if, like him, you're not suited to it.

He walks towards evening
passing a cemetery of stark headstones,
straight-edged and definite,
nothing you could resile from
or avoid in the sudden hot stare
of a November afternoon,
the souls beneath them
exiled from the dusty streets
and goings-on of the town,
lying there at a safe distance from the living.

When you forget nothing,
when everything's recalled
in all its scent and colour and light,
there's no exorcism he knows
except hoarding of letters in his head.
Mostly these thoughts
are the only bits of light in his mind.

He turns his face into the breeze
to decipher its direction,
registers the shift in the wind
now coming from the south east.

It was in the pale limestone country
of the south east that he was born.
So, he fancies he comes from a direction
like a breeze might, wafting in,
picking up the strong scents of the Mallee
and drifting them on across the border.

Now, he walks onwards with head bowed
like a monk working and reworking
some exotic illuminated manuscript
for all his life, Penola's sung to him
words threaded through eucalypts
in a green voice notched down low.

On the Pre-Socratics: Thales versus Heraclitus
Luke Fischer

for my daughter

It's been said that language
separates us from being,
abstracts us from immersion
in immediacy, but witnessing
my daughter learn, I find myself
considering the Pre-Socratics.

I see you dwell in the logos
as a fish in the sea—an encompassing element
virtually imperceptible—though as yet
venturing only as far as your rock pool's boundaries.

Your talent for imitation, its astonishing precision,
assumes the shape of a new expression, 'no way',
uttered on the fly, not intended for your ears,
as trickling water quickly gathers in a groove.

You kick off your shoes just 'like Daddy does',
hold a pen correctly as though you'd attended school and
'write' zigzag letters that are not a bad rendering
of my almost illegible hand, as though our actions
were a coursing river—our bodies its bed—and the water,

remembering, flowed on as a tributary
in what you do—fractal reflections on different scales
as river systems, alveoli, blood vessels, leaf veins
all display the branching patterns of water.

But the clarity of your gaze
suggests a still lake (more than a river),
mirroring the particulars of its surroundings,
wherein we recognise things we hadn't noticed
about ourselves.

You join words
into phrases, sentences,
each distinct yet undivided
as dispersed droplets on a table—
holding the same surface tension—
swiftly reunite in a tiny puddle.

Like a young Nereid
presiding over shoals,
you love to sit in the bath,
scoop and pour water
from vessel to vessel.
In short, confirming Thales:
Everything is water.

Yet the spark in your eyes
and gestures, brightening each day,
how, like a torch, you grasped the word
'light' (and the Arabic *daw* ضَوْء)
and could thenceforth
distinguish the oddest wall lamp
and a chandelier, candles, lanterns and sunshine
as so many instances of the one
'light'—with the fire of the logos
you had lit up that room
in the mansion of forms
housing every possible
illumination.

In quick succession
further referents ignited:
'star', 'moon', 'sun'
'flower', 'stone', 'sculpture'
'water' (soon evaporated), 'table', 'telephone',
enveloped by a spreading wildfire, rose
into the sky as flashing fireflies,
increasing the multitude of stars
that orient your world.

According to water's babble
language is 'acquired'

but tongues of fire declare
every word is seized
by leaping flame, dry wood
devoured until it's wholly fire.

Perhaps the first word you uttered
(even before 'light') was 'no'—
no to the way of opinion
(and the puree we tried to spoonfeed you
as, mouth sealed, you shook your head)—
our way, that of the old gods
soon to be overthrown.

'By yourself!', 'by yourself!'
is your insistent refrain (addressing
yourself from a god's-eye view)
whenever we attempt to lend
a hand—whether in putting on
your shoes or climbing steep stairs—
and, unwaveringly, you make us
redundant in one or another task.

This burning determination
like a spot fire recalls
the defiant wisdom
of Heraclitus, The Obscure
(the Beethoven
of ancient thought)
who having found truth
deposited his manuscript
at the Temple of Artemis
indifferent to whether others
could decipher his riddles.

You were two-and-a-half-feet tall
with an eight-foot personality,
a candle stub with a disproportionate wick,
when speaking with your mother
I named you with the epithet
'the sweet dictator'.

Thus it is manifest: everything is fire!

But I've forgotten to mention 'air':
how you dance on your tippy-toes,
come out of your sleeping-cocoon
and flutter through the living room
as a butterfly.

And your earthiness too:
playing with dirt and sand, or feigning
a tantrum by slowly crawling
as a weary traveller with a burdensome load
then sobbing flat on the ground
until the moment
when you get your way and
rise again like flame, only seeming
to be quenched in ash.

The Boy From The War Veterans' Home
Martin Langford

When they pointed you in from the office –
one toothbrush, one hairbrush, one cap –
the men must have wondered: *This is no place for a boy* –
though when phosgene had scraped out their lungs
they had scarcely been more …

Now they were counting the days as industrial ruins.

Whom you must join too. For TB of the throat. Doctor said.

So they found you a bed
in a ward for the stoics and shades.

Then left you, to lie there, alone.

Did Gran appear? Christmas Eve?
What with your brothers, the farm,
and her own hazing mind…

Pa out on Indian railroads...

No doubt the men tried to help.

But eleven is early to find out
the people you need yield to needs of their own.

That the play you are in
may have no scenes where you're not alone.

When a war artist taught you to render,
form was a first, lifelong gift – though with no-one inside it.

A prayer of engagement. Of breathing through line.

While men drowned from blisters and phlegm.

While the man with no face
walked the man with no limbs in the sun...

While you died more slowly
than anyone else on the clipboard.

At fifteen they signed you back out:

still unhealed:
since nothing was wrong –
had been wrong from the start –
        but in need of a cure.

You watched what the others all did.

You set yourself jaunty, four-square.

But you could not believe you belonged in the room:
that the world had a place
for the boy who could conjure its weight –
who weighed nothing himself.

When *forward* failed,
there was no under-floor to support you –
doubt tumbling loose like a bat-cave of bitterness:
masks pooling out into shallows.

May was your great gift:
your anchor – your 'distaff Picasso'.

But even great loves don't resolve
into platforms for selves.

And so we sold up and sailed south –
where the light might permit one to re-invent outsets.

Where the wound in your luggage
refused to relinquish its right to a mind of its own.

I'm sorry, I'm sorry, you told her.
And she received that as the whole gift it would have been
were it not cruelled by the damage.
What I saw
was pain need not end.

And thus, as I had to, looked *off.*

To get through.

And not to give witness: the curse of the child.

Thank you –
for my sake – and others –
for turning your rage on yourself –
for the rough human sums.

Nature, they say, abhors vacuums.

But nothing Mum did
could have given this nihil a floor:

lost, at your easel,
for somewhere to start –
for motion to enter your hand –
to make up for there being nothing
you needed to draw . . .

Nothing, you'd rasped, *to be said.*

– Something to test, with my life.

If I gave grief,
I was trying for upright.

Then only helplessness:

watching you twitch
from the trenches, redoubts, you had dug –
as the Huntington's bit –
the unselving disease –
that no-one, this time, had picked up.

Facing the Obelisk / Locals / Twelve Bars Blue / Chin-Chin / Drinks
Ian Crittenden

The Oriental, The Cricketer's Arms, Cooks Hill

I sober up from drinking in the Oriental and get drunk again
in the Cricketers Arms, arriving home sometime after midnight.
I've lost my keys, I knock and there's no answer.
Spook's nose is already thundering.
I wander up the hill, and deflect the surf's applause.
For a long time I've hated this body. It's not my own,
it runs around as if it had no final destination.
Late at night the breeze is still, the ocean a phosphorescent weave.
From this time on I'd like to be a small dinghy
floating off the continental shelf, reading the currents.

Basement on Market Street, Newcastle

Bad wine, bad men. You can't get away
quick enough. Both bring me to my knees
with their promise of pleasure ruined
by stinking compromise. The moon is in pieces
on the gauzy river. The pubs are empty,
intensive care is full. I water the bed of vegetables
with my reeking piss. Spook snuffles
among the dandelions and chilli.
Such abundance, but nothing I can eat.

The Wicko, Wickham

Bad poets are like bad wine. They stick
in your craw, a fishbone swallowed backwards.
I can't not go through with it,
I just have to go on gagging.
If you see me drunk at the poets' pub,
don't slap me on the back.
Just let me pass out, then wake up
sober as the cleaners go through the place.

Sunnyside Tavern, Broadmeadow

It's Grand Final eve and I have no family near,
but I have tears like Gary Martine's sweat.
Since there is someone who burns up the street,
I can only presume that life goes on.
I imagine the two teams toss
and turn in their anticipatory dreams.
Tomorrow, the shield will be lifted,
the battered champions and their drunk fans
toasting the dwindling moon, the dying stars.

The Empire, West Newcastle

I never could keep my big trap shut, bragging
over a schooner in the Empire. Smokes
and tats could never get enough of that flatulence.
Now I've really got something to trumpet:
the critics all think I'm a dickhead! Well,
that's the turd calling the cowpat dirty. Bring it!
I've only got this glass of wine, now,
hedged between me and eternity.

Horseshoe Beach, Newcastle East

A six-pack and baited rod on Horseshoe Beach:
I'm blind again from our river's shimmer,
the ochre sunlight athwart the silos.
The tide runs in, my hooked prawn drifts,
the talk is of the filling morgues. There's another
six-pack in the esky, we're not leaving
until it's gone. The ferry shuffles to Stockton
then back across the abject harbour.
Even through my regret, studying the Way so late,
I'm just as good at composing poems as them.

Home. Islington

The ambitious canary wants to suck seed,
I just want to suck piss and toast the tree frogs
in my back yard. They're kicking up a fuss
again, with a call like a brushtail possum.
The full moon carves out my shadow
which wobbles against the wall. It toasts
me. The moon? A passing cloud dissolves it.

Foghorn Brewhouse, Newcastle

What is the use of so many nearly identical beers?
What is the true minutiae of difference?
In the great transformation, a virus becomes almost human,
one beer becomes a conversation, another turns into
the fish escorting an orphaned supertanker home,
the coal in the supertanker ends up back in a leaf
in a dying forest. Drink up, there's work to do!

Town Hall, Waratah

Three mobility scooters confer on the path
outside the Town Hall. Inside, Waratah's rising aldermen
debate the day's urgent questions.
Who is to say they haven't found the Way?

Lass O'Gowrie, Wickham

Washing my son's hair
in the tapwater at the back of the Lass
I hope that he grows up a talentless drunk,
unlike me, whose little shard of talent
has just made me miserable.
I read their poetry but can't understand a word.
I want my son to be stupid, so he can be raised up, too,
high on the vertical banners of praise!

Hunter Valley Wine Tasting, Lovedale

What are the clouds doing behind the screen
of mountains? Is it smoke piled into burning cumulus,
falling on the plain as ash, as black leaves?
The sun, also, has dropped there,
Light from some headlamps needles down,
suggesting a way out through the hairpins.

Cellar Door 1, Pokolbin

In the witching hour, when I climb inside
the third bottle, I think of that lickspittle
megalomaniac who places his head in the laps
of the powerful, then flaunts their praise
as he climbs ever higher, showing his naked arse.
Keep climbing, ant! May your ambition give you
comfort, even as it suffocates the rest of us:
I read your poetry, dull dishwater,
so cold even the suds have fled. The jonquils
at the cellar door keep blooming.

Kooragang Island

"All the cunts are at the festival
listening to the other cunts read. Poor me,
oh watch me wringing my hands, oh watch my cock
expand as I recite myself. I'm seeing them off
from Kooragang, watching the white egrets
hatch. No regrets here, just the heartbeat
of crickets, the exhaling cloud of gnats,
the mozzies as annoying as those poets",
is what he was reported as saying,
ripping another can of bespoke beer open.

Hexham Bowling Club, Hexham

Birds strung out along the fence
pass for heads on pikes at the edge of town.
The creeks, the rivers, are broken.
Wire between the poles, the palings, twangs.
Choreopsis mocks the freeway with its laughter.
I drive through it, drunk again and surly.
I've ditched my gods for the book of shadows,
and if the index is anything to go by
I'll soon be arriving in hell.

Hunter on Hunter, Newcastle

At Hunter on Hunter midnight's acoustic
duo pretend to take requests and each
sip from a middy of wine: him white, her sparkling red.
A short, angry emperor bustles out on his phone,
dark tarmac hissing with Marly wheeze and soothed
with slow blinkers, arcs from his red-boxed milds.
Ancient tunes trickle onto the street, wind kicks
around a juice box. Will I ever get to see your face again?

Belmont 16 Foot Sailing Club. Belmont

Past the Sixteen Footers, small boats,
skip under the Watagans' long shade,
a hundred, it looks like – my mounting
drunkenness, my balance all shimmy.
The handrail glints, still, and the distant
carpark's disdain manifests as rain.
Back inside, then, leave the forecourt.
Mind sails south a moment, past Swansea.

The Windsor Castle. East Maitland

They always say they want the best
for the kids, and fret over measures
of intelligence. My brain and its, um,
"chemistry", have screwed my life up.
Look instead at the sudden mill of cash
at the Bradford, the Windsor Castle –
these snotty cherubs, will they inherit dot coms, soft
drink domains, run for a seat on the Council?
You know they will, so why bother asking.

The Premier Hotel, Broadmeadow

Each bar performs my sadness. It crescendoes
by design. I philandered widely, a lover in every port.
'I'm only attracted to strong women. But then I get scared
and run away.' I cracked open families
to egg myself on. Now I'm exiled from this town
by my tastes. On the way out, there's The Premier,
that pub at the sharp end of the nineways:
the first stop always ends up the last.

Cellar Door 2. Pokolbin

This morning's glary frost on the couchgrass,
the bare queue of Pokolbin's poplars.
Stay inside, unless: we're all hermits now.
Who do I talk to? Is messenger even secure?
These books of his – are they saying what they seem
to say? I'd drift deliberately west, but how, and how
would I know what was waiting there? The hungry wastes.
What use are peers, friends, family, so far apart?
A thousand years of quarantine, thirty of drunken exile.
Wipe down the glass, look through the window.
I started out late, a little unadvantaged. So?

The Delaney, Cooks Hill

What the world has taken away from me
has been given back to others. Just accept it,
it's easier that way, I don't want to work
I just want to drink, plunder a book in the midsummer shade
of a lazy park or garden. Eventually, those words
will drift off into cirrus, stratus, cumulonimbus
freighting themselves inland. For now, though, the drought
continues, cremating the continent, doubting species
into extinction. How I wish I could gently stab
the faces of all the climate change deniers –
not that it would make much difference. It's a party-
political knife-fight: instinct, gut. I'll stay the course, implacable.

General Roberts Hotel, New Lambton

Wine in the sunshine, flicking between sutras
and *The Best Australian Poetry 2011*.
I walk down to the gully, watch the light
drift past the flash of wild orchids. How little
ambition I have, how fun it is having it, and how
awkward it sometimes is, not explaining it well.
People rate Lambton Heights, the view,
but I'll sit here in the front bar window.

The Albion Hotel, Singleton

I don't mean to, but I claim the bottlo's
back alley with this stinking piss. Steam rises into
that winking slot of neon and mist drops
up into first light, dawn's river's swash.
How many times have I come this way
against the afternoon's streaming sun, slinking
down lanes, avoiding those chattering neighbours.
Am I so settled in my ways? I've wet my feet.

Remembering Iraklion
Ross Gillett

The ship's wake
simmered down as it fanned out.

We were letting everything slip away behind us.
Cities, islands, other lovers.

*

Our destination came alongside at sunrise.
It was shedding darkness
from rooftops and roads.

When the ferry stopped its shuddering
Iraklion bumped against us.

*

We almost had the dawn streets
to our long-shadowed selves.

There was a man
pushing his broom with a sly lightness of touch.

He seemed half asleep
but he gave us a wink,
a blessing almost too quick to catch.

*

In Lion Square
our rucksacks leaned together
on a stone step,
two battered canvas torsos.

My fellow traveller,
all faded blue jeans and fierce blue eyes,
stood guard as I scouted for rooms.

Fountain beasts watched over her,
lions carved by someone who had never seen a lion.
Never-ending streams of water
flowed from their open mouths.

An image of eternity.
A poor substitute for a roar.

*

The door of one hotel was not quite closed.
I took that narrow strip of darkness at its word.

The reception desk
was a tourist altar.
Plaster saint,
pen and register on chains
and a bell.

The deity appeared feet-first
down steep stairs.
He wore tight robes,
a fisherman's jumper and suit trousers
pulled on over pyjamas.

*

The staircase was the twisted
eye of a needle,
a stretched gate.

We squeezed through
into a dingy rented heaven
with a view of the harbour of Heracles.

*

From our one window
we could see the ship cranes dip and swing.

We were safe
from all that departure,
all that arrival.

*

That night, the dust storm,
an airborne desert coming for Iraklion.
Grains of the Sahara piled up on the windowsill.

In the morning our harbour outlook
was lost in a parched mist.

*

We saw the dimmed greatness of Iraklion.
An arid glory
draped the city in its veils.

Our refuge from the withering storm
was a crooked room
and a mattress so old and soft
lying down was falling into one another.

We left Iraklion to its faded fate.

*

The dust was with us in the Cretan streets,
a gritty benediction.

My lover waved to me
from the end of a clouded street
in the faintly invaded city.

She beckoned with both arms.
She was a swimmer in the dust.

*

What sort of truth was it,
that vagueness at the window?

Something vast was in the air.

The sky was a dull glow at the end of every street.
We walked the breakwater
and saw an earth-coloured surf.

*

In my dream
the lions are coming home.
A fountain follows them and turns into more lions.

We are both there
waiting for lions.

*

When the miracle of the dust ended,
on a day when the wind had nothing more to give,
we drove to a treeless beach.

It was a day for distances.

The sea was a flat enormous presence
drawing a line under the sky.
The afternoon went for miles in all directions.

We lay on the forgiving sand
and slipped into each other's lives.

*

The rain remembered Iraklion.
It sloped in from the west
and a darkness gleamed in the streets.

The dust went to sea
and from the breakwater
we watched a cloudiness depart.

We were lovers
staring into a flowering tide.

*

These streets, these memories,
as if there's a way through
the haze of time.

In the blink of an eye
we were swept up
and emptied into each other's arms.

The god of small hotels
grudged us a key.

The harbour signalled
while the room embraced us.

A beach became an anchorage.

*

It was all a strangeness
breeding certainties between us.

Even the dust
was a way of seeing.

We kept the key.

Staying home
Caroline Williamson

'the silence in Australia is intense, even in the city'
– Prithvi Varatharajan, 'Travel Lessons'

At this point there is a kind of jamming – I did
make a list but everything is crying out
for attention. The garden: couch grass and tradescantia
roaring back, surrounding the little perennials I planted
last year, gorging on their food. Half an hour
on this cool sunny afternoon would be useful,
a good start, half an hour is what the garden
needs every day and doesn't get, why not
when there's so much unoccupied time? Yesterday
I decided on a walk every morning. This morning
the walk was postponed till after breakfast in order
to take the dog after his breakfast which invariably
happens after humans have eaten. But the dog
cut his paw yesterday leaping across a rocky stream
in the Darebin Parklands and we decide he needs rest
so I head off alone north into brilliant sunlight
and round to the creek, stopping only for a photo
of the half-built bridge and also to pick up oranges
and a loaf of bread from the wholefood shop, then home
to second coffee. Sit down for a bit with Twitter.
Observe the impossibility of thoughtfulness in however many
characters when it comes to sex and gender: which side
are you on is all. I am remembering a beautiful
photo of young lovers: trans man and cis woman if we
have to use that language, posted two days ago
and now irretrievably lost to me, while at the same time
I am trying and failing to list every single one
of the varied sexual assaults that have blighted my life,
and also I am thinking that all of this should be possible
to deal with, given time for conversations
and skill in listening. Meanwhile there's my own bread
on the way, sourdough starter still refusing to rise,
only a matter of time. Maybe tomorrow evening
there'll be new delicious heavy bread, not well shaped
but nobody complaining. I was going to trace

a pattern from my new book from Japan: the simple
loose top, no darts, no separate sleeves, see how it goes,
excavate the fabric stash for something forgotten,
machine the side seams, finish the edges by hand,
and also there's his jumper half darned, my new skill
but that is for the evening: darning and Masterchef,
three humans and two animals congregating
in the living room. There's a pile of my socks for sorting,
a pile of jeans and track pants and trousers
for folding and putting away. There is dust
accumulating everywhere. There is also family history
- a summary half written, an hour or two a day
would knock it over in a fortnight. A photo
from before the first world war, out of four grandparents
the only one with a camera. The grandmother,
her little brothers and sisters, her cheerful parents
all lined up in their windy garden. Emails to write,
neglected friends. And no time made today,
this leisurely sunny day, for the main business,
the dreaming mind, the hand scribbling on paper
to catch something barely there, whisking
past in the dailiness of it all, unreachable
thirty seconds later. Twitter is saying how in Bristol, England,
after years of futile campaigning, people have turned
to ropes and a big crowd and took down the slaver's statue.
People are marching in America – socially distant
wherever possible. A baker in California, famous
for her recipe books, is Instagramming the faces
and contact details of black people who bake
bread, pies, cakes, tarts, biscuits –
this one is also a cellist. We made a donation,
we put an Aboriginal sticker on our gatepost,
we know that is not enough. Sometimes
this week I have been craving libraries open
to all and sundry for however long they want
to sit and scribble – even a coffee shop, a table
at a safe distance from others, space outside this house.
Twitter is telling me that cabin fever is the affliction
of the week, three months and counting, sharing
meals with good friends in our home or theirs
is lovely but not enough, we want the casual

contact with strangers, the crowded tram, the shop
busy with customers. I need elastic for masks, head off
daringly to the fabric shop. Wait in the socially distanced
queue at the door, they are counting their visitors
out and in, directing us to the enormous bottle
of hand sanitiser on the counter. Back home
with my new elastic and old scraps I go into action:
masks are small but fiddly. Whatever it is I need
in my life right now, there ought to be a list,
comprehensive, with priorities in order, a day
mapped out in advance. The balance of household,
body and mind. How is it possible for a whole
morning, a whole day, to slip through my fingers
in a drift of inattention, falling into sadness?

Woman is the Cow of the World
Maria Vouis

Udder and tit, meat and trade she is it, picked over and laid, everyday
chattel and like her pretty sister cattle, she is driven,
riven, ploughed, sucked, trafficked and trucked, woman is the cow of the world.

Labia majora razored to minor, surgically sculpted little girl flowers,
cut for Web porn doctors define her, uploaded midnight to dawn
hour by hour, hopeful checkout chick splayed on the casting couch of lick-dick,
revolver between her tits or up her vulva, princess of gun pornography,
her body a cartography of man's squirt and grunt, woman is the cow of the world.

Pressed mute in pages of the Bible, on the left side of churches,
swept from priestess to prostitute by a scratch of Pope Gregory's pen,
holy oracle to hole, abbess to scrubber in the Magdalen laundries, vessel of God
to unwed mother-bitch, healer to stripped, scorched witch, woman is the cow of the world.

Woman is the tart with or without heart, the whore with more
on all fours, waste of space when her dugs stretch to the floor, jiggling milk
in lap dancer blue-veined jugs, nipple frothing under lace, aching to feed
an infant mouth in need at home alone, woman is the cow of the world.

Woman is   the pack-animal lugging   water, dung,   and her family honour,
black burqa spectres with   letter box faces,   amber eyes   written in khol,
mailing   panicked messages,   sisters snuffed-out by   silk pillows squashed
in the mitts   of her brothers   who creep away   lawless as shadows
to pray   at the mosque beside her unnamed lover,   woman is the cow of the world.

Woman is   the bleeder,   the breeder,   the walking   womb
sperm bank   with no Super-scheme,   penned quietly in   suburban   nurseries,
babbling   to babies   losing   her place   in the money race,
losing   her figure   then   her mind,   woman is the cow of the world.

Murdered wives,   uncounted each week,   by the loves of their lives,   corpses can't speak
of pets butchered   in practice runs,   children's bodies   hung on their breasts
with the sob frozen on their last breath,   so few arrests,   woman is the cow of the world.

War-raped,   sewn on mass   with   soldiers' seed   so   her new-born's faces
flag   her captors' races   and tap her labour,   horizontal slavery,
fecund engine pumping generations   of   battle butchered boys.   No, not news.
But true,   today   as   always,   woman,   is, the cow of the world.

Dust
Damen O'Brien

"I will show you fear in a handful of dust."
– TS Elliot, The Waste Land

1.

Libya stains its neighbours with a blush of uprooted dust,
the bloody sunsets of apocalypse and the wilting dismay of
crops dying. Life and death. Soil can't be made, they proved
that in some lab long ago. There is something indefinable
in the regolith that can't be replicated, some secret magic
powder clobbered loose from dandruffed Tinkerbells.
From space, Libya blanches and dries, and its neighbours
rejoice from rich pickings sifting down to dust their crops.
The mouth of the Amazon far away boils with a brown slab
of Brazil, cut from the banks and slides and alligator rushes
every year, scooped out of the sides of old volcanoes to stir
out to sea with the kelp and the busy sharks. In the year of winter
when Krakatoa blew, the ejecta tuffed and sneezing into sleet
was the shape of death and portents and mortality's reminder.
Now trees grow on its wounded flanks and the monster sleeps.
The world's net, scooping solar wind has repeatedly snagged
crushed meteors and star stuff, and from them life came once,
so the theory goes. Next time, the smoke palling out of space
may be a bruising spray of meteors and the dust will take us.

2.

In the Archives room, the papers are eared and worn, smeared
with a reader's grip. My marks are there –ultra-violet betrayal
of fingerprints and grime, caking the keyboard, crumbing
on the words, flakes of old outmoded messages, flecks of thought.
We're moving to a 'paperless office', consigning the mullock heap
of carbon into history. The photocopy boys rejoice. The shredder
monkeys lay down their friable reams and wash their hands of whiteout.
Filters suck the tang of pollen and disgruntlement out of the office,
comb esters out of the air, catch our mingled disappointments,
the grey transactions, coups and short term gains of business.
Now fingertips are going on-line, and breadcrumbs are shed,
or syphoned there. But these are new particles, cross-cut
out of a new wind and we old serfs still drop our dying cells,
share our ageless and shabby atoms and rebreathe the austere air.
The next filter upgrade, taking pathogens out of the atmosphere,
insurrection out of our minds, lunchbreaks out of our contracts,
spam out of our inbox, may suck up the grit of us in one hoarse gulp,
one backspace, click, delete and nothing will pass through its matrix.

3.

The dust is billowing redly over the container terminal
as articulated trucks shovel containers into its mouth.
In these backlot suburbs there is always a low animal groaning
of freight trains spreading a weekly crop of coal dust,
a charcoal patina to outdoor tables and to asthma lungs.
Here, the mangroves give way to the shaved and torn pelt of
building sites, burnt stubble, open workings and raw dirt.
There is a coked breath rising from each contribution,
entwining and brewing, coating houses with invisible spores.
We are shaken with the spillage of our lives,
the shed detritus of things: the leaves, the hair, the
snowing smoke and matt of men and cats and dogs.
All these things seem pounded in a heartless mortar:
the glass sky, sharp and ragged as a shark's tooth,
the terracotta and ceramic clot of earthy earth, and
between them nothing but an accumulation of dust;
the worship of dust; or baking, flawed cities of dust;
the civilisations pullulating and sweating out of dust
and returning to it, like poor claymation caricatures.

4.

How do we forgive our odours and exhalations?
The residues and sediments that salt and smear
the backwaters and cul-de-sacs of our veins?
The crystals knapping and sharding in each joint?
In the heavy spongey polyps of our cerebellum,
a suspension of plaque accumulates and
time makes its inevitable dissolves of our body.
we are sanded back to pith, and stain, and dust.
Remember man, the priest recites, *that you are dirt*:
spring saplings loamed and aggregated from the earth
to wear a temporary robe of greenery and life,
fated to be cut back to the stump that lifted us up,
the sawdust spattering the soil. But we need no
reminders: the taste of iron in the sandpaper wind
blowing through the wastelands of our bodies.
Our skin twitches with dead cells sloughing
and the weeping chrism of each pore and hair.
Nothing permanent can be attempted. Nothing in the
long average of infinity can be done to clean the world.

5.

The slow wearing and weathering down of time-
the eagle sharpening its beak on shapeless hills:
all drifts of dust, and subtle erosions.
On Titan and on Ganymede, and the barren Moon,
the long reward for steadfast creaking around the Sun
is wasted pits and seeps and frozen seas of dust.
A softening of edges: the gentle breeze has
worn away the haft of the axe, and etched at the blade.
We are granted a vision of the suffocating
end of days, when all things put aside and stored
wear down, and the flatlands creep and swirl.
The afterlife is just as dry and pitiless, we suspect
as some gewgaw left languishing on a shelf
fuzzed with the fine cilia of air falling in a still
room forever. All dull brilliance and musty pearl:
hamster wheels and Hades, thirsty lands that wait
for clouds to build and hammer clay. Purgatory
without remorse. Heaven without redemption.

6.

It's on my mind today: the one last permanent thing,
that survives even after cockroaches and scavengers
get their final come-uppance. Smallest reductions possible.
Ur-particles: the scraps from the philosopher's quest
to carve the universe into smaller bits –kernels and specks
and other ontological leftovers defying classification. Atoms
of doubt. Peppercorns of despair. Grains of uncertainty.
First principles and prime movers: intangibles and axioms.
However finely powdered, these yield no flash or bang.
What does? Not my works. Cleaning the house today
is an exercise in futility. Entropy is winning.
Each expenditure of energy is a small failure,
the world cools and tomorrow the dirt accretes again.
Nature abhors a vacuum and punishes its accomplishments:
all my rearrangements of the dust, all my wheezy bags.
My unswept floors are cast and sprayed with the same matter
that makes up the blousy fire of the cosmos. No doubt,
nature hates my duster too, and places behind me new grains
to coat each work, as if to say, *all of this too is dust.*

Dry as a Pom's Towel
Tug Dumbly

He wanted to go, and my job to keep him on,
to drive the husk of his body from his house
to beach and park bench, to feed the birds,
to see the sea, scenes he could no longer frame
with any joy from the four corners of his walker.

He just wanted home, and the Bermuda Triangle
of his ageing – bed, breakfast table, lounge, and then back
to oblivion of sheets. He just wanted to sleep.

I'd coax him to the crossword, over his rhubarb and yogurt.
He'd sometimes play along. Funeral speech. Six letters: Eulogy.
But to force him to any activity, the rudest scaffolding of life –
shower, dress, toilet, food – seemed a Sisyphean cruelty.
I'd wheedle, bribe, bully and plea to oyster him from his 'settee',
blast the Toreador Song from his beloved Carmen
to try and get him up and keep my contract with his family.

No dignity in ageing. What did he care?
It was the sheer effort he bucked, the exhaustion
of just contemplating this gnattish stuff.
I counted it a victory to clean him up, to change
the sodden kilo of his pads, or shave his crenelated face.
To dab and scrape at each sallow gulch of stubble,
to rinse the razor of his white neck tufts,
was the gloved agony of preserving a ruined painting.

Stark ears jugged to parchment skull, he was
Dobell's Joshua Smith, only shrunker, more caricatured.
His skin wept and bruised like turning fruit,
his teeth a shipwreck you tried to escape.
Then the weekly battle of the shower and his howl
at the scald of tepid water. Though once seated
he'd give a pleasured moan
as I soaped the dunes of his backbone.

After this, I'd say, we'll go for a drive.
But why? he'd say. Why? I don't want to go anywhere.
And go to see what – more cars, trees, streets? Oh goody! …

As I drove him to sarcasm I privately agreed.
He was so fucken polite it hurt my heart
with questions of where a shoulder ends
and a neck starts, or a mountain,
and when is the climb not worth the while,
and why? And once again why?

I loved him, and he might have loved me,
his companionable torturer.
Hard to fit the remnant I knew
with the man I met at his White Lady funeral.
The program pictured a stranger's face
fleshed in vigour, buoyed on food and drink
in Ibiza, or some other brightly bronzed place.
The speakers extolled the orthopaedic genius,
the philanthropist, the carpenter,
the farmer, husband and father.

His daughter thanked me. I felt a fool
for how I'd treated like a child
this surgeon and sentient being,
with all his precision, feeling and history
packed liked dominos inside.
I lined up, put a rose on his box
and apologised. Then filed out
to the tearjerker Time to Say Goodbye.
He got his wish and now he's gone home,
to his farm in Wales, to his friends, to his wife,
to his whole other life.

The Babel of Rites
Syros
John Foulcher

1

Kristof's house is a clutter
of bunkers
along the side of the hill,
so it appears
this is a cliff, and these are caves
in which we live.
From our room, you must go out in the heat,
walk down a few steps
to the kitchen
gouged from stone.
When the windows are open,
the wind throws
everything about,
and the shutters clatter like maracas.
Below, Ermoupolis
is fanned by the deep blue bay
where lumbering ferries wade in from the Aegean,
as blue as the Aegean would be.
Kristof has painted
the ceilings blue.
When you lie back on the bed
there is a sky above,
a ceiling beyond,
and your body feels like a sack
made from skin.
The stairs you will take to Ermoupolis
are hewn from marble
and stone, they are worn
so smooth, like skin
on the hill's body, the body's hill.

2

Waking early, the heat feeling its way
into the room, I read about Mary Magdalene:
after the carcase of Golgotha, there was nothing
inside her body, though only her body
made sense, as she came alone to the tomb.
The gardener was there, doing a gardener's job,
as if the tomb were another garden, as if
he were planting something. *Please* she asked
let me have back what I have loved. Then
he raised his hand, and she knew heat in her body,
though the skin was untouched between them.
She ran with the news and told no one,
she ran in her body, down the side of the hill.

3

Our neighbour, who's eighty-seven,
has been twenty years free of a husband.
Painted white and olive-green, her house
nudges the ochre of Kristof's house.
There's a calm there, in those colours.
Most days she perches at the window,
her phone in her hand. We hear her talking,
a frantic, high-pitched sling of words
we don't understand, though she speaks
with the lilt of clouds, the unforgiving sky.
Her daughters come each day with meals
and news. They don't tell her everything.
They don't talk of her son, who has cancer,
though she hears between words, there's nothing
of comfort in silence. She will never go down
to Ermoupolis. Here she is close to the sun.
Her name is Elpida, which in English means *hope*.

4

Walking down
through Ano Syros,
on the stairs made of marble and stone.

All paths will lead to the sea,
I believe,
but soon there is nothing here
quaint or familiar,
only stray children
and thin, scribbled cats.
The heat is a silky blue wave from the Aegean.
I sit down, check my map,
find I'm nowhere.
But all roads will lead to the sea
I believe,
so I go down, still,
coming at last to a sea
of tourists and talk, cafés and shady boulevards.
Above me,
the houses of Ano Syros
are elaborations.
I sit for a while and think about
going up,
how hard this will be,
the atonement
of my slow steps to the sky.
If it weren't so
pedestrian, you would think
of gates and choruses, at the end of these infinite stairs.

5

While the young laze on the sand
in bronze relief, we lug our old bodies
into the tired Aegean. Already the sun
is sidling away, into a sea the colour
of stone. I think of the Korai, those
pale stone women of the Acropolis.
They smile, though their eyes are as absent
as suns. The Persians smashed them
to fragments but couldn't wipe the smiles
from their faces, the currents of blue
from their gowns, the crimson folds.
The waves are like their draped chitons,
lapping the pebbles on this beach.

We haul ourselves over the sand, towel
our bodies dry. The folds of your dress, my shirt.

6

On this rocky hill, a church lower
than only the sky. Under the sun,
it looks like a kind of predator,
lording it over the houses below,
those houses that have been thrown
down. Nothing is deeper than the sea-blue
sky that hovers over its sky-blue dome.
The priest is Polish, and he struggles
with the texts, though his homily
seems unleashed. A man in black
with his back to us leads the liturgy.
We sit in a cloud of unknowing,
searching for something familiar,
something that could be enough.
I scan the walls, where the saints
are faultless. Outside, wind. The service
goes on, like the rush of wind,
and I recognise only the Babel of rites –
Kyrie Eleison, amen, hallelujah.
Below the mural Mass, the rest
is sound, undiminished by words. That
slumped, Hellenic Christ, hanging there.

7

On our last morning in Syros,
Kristof leads us
to the rooftop.
We watch sun dragging itself from the sea,
shrouded in clouds
as thin as dust.
Blood-red, it comes between crosses,
the Orthodox and Catholics
lapped in its light.
I think once more of Mary Magdalene
lying in the heat,

dawn crawling
bloodied and beaten
into her room. I see her standing at the window,
touching her belly, her breasts,
scanning the sun-struck hills,
the blue shreds of sky,
then going down
into the dark. *Beautiful,
yes?* says Kristof, and we go down, into the dark.

Squall
Anthony Lawrence

1

Among the disciplined carriers of breaking news, intimate
broadcasts from the lattice-
      work of wind & rain,
            death notices & unveiled suggestions of harm
such as when the tarantula wasp consigns the drone
of its scouting flight
      to an ambush predator's stronghold,
           the trapdoor spider's burrow or the tunnel
of the furrow worm, there is one who offers the manifesto
or missive equal weight:
      the Messenger moth,
           its feelers fishbone ferns, its wing-powder
thumbed across polished name plates on a Columbarium.
Somewhere, a snow-dome
      featuring a horse in harness,
           silver bells, & a moth fighting extremes
of weather, is being shaken. What is spoken aloud remains
in the jurisdictions
      of memory, the close-
           knit parishes of wild association.

2

Of memory & peripheral sight, of what is there
& what has been,
      in a summer lane, perhaps,
           hemmed-in by flowering vine & thorn,
the makings of fright & adrenalin gain currency:
the currawong,
      that beak with eyes
           who learned the two-tone whistle & refrain
from hearing death-metal on repeat from the attic
of a deceased estate.
      The skitter of rats
           in a rhombus of nightshade, stamen & pistil
tainted for the curious who lean in to part the undergrowth

        & taste their own
                time-lapse fall
                        like gravity in a recording of a honey spill.
Of intent, find a winter lane with dying stag horns
& army worms
        that have made it down
                from as far as the sugarcane districts
to cripple the engine rooms in heads of corn.
The lane might be
        a Still Life with Do Not Resuscitate
                on the exit gate.

3

Regarding the man given six to eight months,
or as he suggested,
        accurately
                as it turned out, *an indeterminate*
amount of time to lever living from the commonplace,
he often surprised himself
        by tickling his own side
                & feet, & then there was the diagnosis,
like an aerial view, with commentary, of a loading race
at the entrance
        to a euphemism
                for meat works, with doomed animals
encouraged, via electric prods & yelled abuse, to enter.
The man had a landscape
        photographer's eye
                for composition. He could frame a mountain
range with smithereens of smoke blowing into frame
to give a scene
        the kind of melancholy edge
                you'd expect to find if Hopper's 'Night Hawks
at the Diner' had been coupled with a video of bottle-nose
dolphins, at Sea World,
        eating paint from the pool side
                & dying of blown hearts during a tail-walk.
The man entered a yurt to begin a nine day Vipassana
as he'd heard that sitting
        for long spells without goals

     might just be the tripwire with which to snare
& end anxiety. The yurt had a pitted roof, low ceilings
& no windows
  like a cockroach bait, he said
     to the first person he met.
While extended time in silence might be fine
for the snow leopard,
  without the distractions
     of talk & animated expression, the man went
looking for action & found it in daydreams of a tri-hull
catamaran, island-hopping
  through Indoanywhere.
     Things did not go well. First he hyper-
ventilated like a frigate bird flying its red balloon,
then he lay
  among meditators
     who were forced to surface like subs
& confront his need to vanish like emulsion film
in a digital world.
  A lace curtain rose & fell
     as he was dismissed
like a thought from a crowded waiting room of the mind.

4

Listening to the Moody Blues, your mother drops a stitch
& swears in what is now
  a lost Outer Hebridean dialect.
     Needled, a red cable sweater is a time capsule,
the wool riddled with lanolin & blackberry dye. In her day
it was Rex Harrison
  spinning on a '78
     & everyone in flame light over their hobbies,
listening. On the wall, an out-of-focus photo of a woman
in tennis clothes
  lying along the back of a man
     in a leather jacket, war-ace helmet & goggles,
flying his Norton Commando down a country road.
Your mother talks
  about riding pillion
     in a blur of speed as though it involved

minimal risk. Her features alternate between reflection
& regret
      as orange light
           animates the sweater's progress in her hands.

5

Under the stained glass cover of a porch light, throwing
a lapsed inventory
      of shadows, a Messenger moth
           leaves instructions for how to process grief
in code on the wall. Snow begins to fall as a harness bell
rings somewhere near.
      Memory is a dome
           we shake until the past settles down or spills
from fissures that appear each time we remember.
Solitude defies capture
      on film or music score,
           & personal growth might be a cabled sweater
grained with firelight in a Nineteen Fifties living room.
A motorbike backfires
      in a blacked-out lane
           at the end of a thought. A woman watches
a moth land on her arm. A field organ in a folk song
competes with My Fair Lady
      as a home-movie
           of a funeral cortege lights the room with aqua-
marine. A squall can be a storm or cry, heard simultaneously.

Colasion
Ian Crittenden

There's fuckery afoot. The street I want to turn into
is blocked off by a police car, bi-flashing-polar.
An Imperial Stormtrooper helmet, a Corolla
hatchback hurries past the boarded-up Town Hall,
away towards the stunted pines lining the oval, receding
then disappearing into dusk. Leaflets blow in a data-storm
and the last fingers of sunlight strum
the trees, the fences, in air as moist as a sea.

Black clouds, spilt toner.
Rain gauzes the next suburb.
It's nearing the middle of winter:
pigeon-hued clouds border Rorschachs
of depressive cumuli, squat on the tree-lined horizon.
It's a patchwork of cold inertia, of darkening
and damp fustiness: my mind
is the business blowing through it,
the apophenic shapes, fragmented puddles.

Apophenic shapes in a hoarsening shit storm
appear in the headlit haloes of trees. The view
from forty thousand feet is a kind of corporate catascopia:
those shining crowns, the rising steam,
the ant-work of traffic and cold cubes of tofu
and at the edges, on the post-industrial fringe,
waves release a thistling spray above
the redacted shapes of silvery shadows.
And, to the west, the crimson rim of the dying world
where corporations end, and grow back, up, and out.

Endlessly, the corporations lattice the city
to which I return like a dog to its vomit.
There's rain thick as shredded documents
shaken from windows, filling the street,
and the faint stink of entitlement thwarted
as businesses collapse like The Odradek Stadium.
Snails riddle hydrangea leaves, making green colanders.
Stars seed the night with their ancient capital.

Ancient capitals lit with neon, smoke and bandwidth.
Should we dismantle poetry now, and will it be replaced
with something better? How do we put it back together?
Fucking in the afternoon, drinking margaritas,
and eating margheritas, and reading *The Master
and Margarita* and licking the jade tableware?
The aim is to go nowhere, while going everywhere.
Spring is pilling Laman Street's empty trees
which nod in disagreement with the wind.

Nodding disagreement, the small child glowers,
a malevolent robot chomping empty air.
A fake American accent is quite common
among children, anal is preferred by adolescent boys,
giving mainly, but receiving also,
and then there is the Beresfield Bow-tie
and the sexual possibilities of they-on-they.
Dysphoric plane tree fuzz fills the air.
Legs spread, hands on the roofs of their SUVs,
the callow knowingness of hoodied housos, searched.

Out of the houso place, hauling the filing cabinets whole,
holding their heavy lives, the officers look just stoked.
Unshredded lives are shredded, a fist to the solar plexus,
suspect foliage drenched in the flexing rain.
There are older fragmentations not to do with age
but fortitude, the self that does not heal
but calves in the sun like a glacier
sun-pricked and collapsing into the sea.

The sea collapses against the sea wall and again
inside itself like a party or a calendar
from a cooler year, rotting out in the shed.
Mushrooms burgeon on the lawn, the pine bark
molders and the soldier ants flense a desiccated skink
so that all that's left is tinnitus and air.

Tinnitus and rain: wet sirens
blocking the street at each end. Laundered
leaves flash blue and red in the darkness.

The sky's tattooed with scattered clouds
empurpled by the city's glow, plump with rain.
Each square of the footpath is promising as an empty cell
in a spreadsheet. A Rum Corps meditation.

A quick bundy and coke as the tattooist skitters
her art across their skin: a verse from the Koran
or a headline from El Telegraph?; it's possible
those characters spelling bàndītóu
could mean 'lower your head in manure';
the purple blush on plumpish thighs
is just for you. My only tats:
on the backs of my eyes, the profit
and loss, the liability, limited, of Colasion.

Strelitzias and chaos: rising inequality
in these planters filled with weeds. Artless
frontages promise no more
than a co-star spot in the magnitude of space
with a cheesy credit, a string of nothingness.
Rain beads on the tricolor paddywagons.
I suppose I'll come back later, take a long ride
on my murdercycle. I might reconsider my position
on brand awareness, risk aversion,
their artful collusions, evasions.